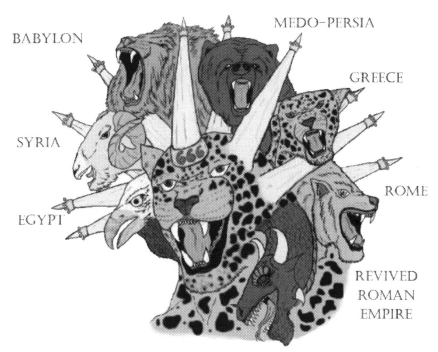

BABYLON

MEDO-PERSIA

GREECE

SYRIA

ROME

EGYPT

REVIVED
ROMAN
EMPIRE

REVELATION 13:8

"REVELATION"
The Patmos Vision Unveiled

REV. GERALD F. MCPETERS

WESTBOW·
PRESS
A DIVISION OF THOMAS NELSON
& ZONDERVAN

WestBow Press books may be ordered through booksellers or by contacting:

WestBow Press
A Division of Thomas Nelson & Zondervan
1663 Liberty Drive
Bloomington, IN 47403
www.westbowpress.com
1 (866) 928-1240

Scripture taken from the King James Version of the Bible.

ISBN: 978-1-4908-6822-6 (sc)
ISBN: 978-1-4908-6823-3 (hc)
ISBN: 978-1-4908-7071-7 (e)

Library of Congress Control Number: 2015902685

Print information available on the last page.

WestBow Press rev. date: 3/13/2015

ACKNOWLEDGEMENTS

I would like first of all to acknowledge God, for the love He has given me for his word, and for the call of God on my life. I would also, like to acknowledge my Christian wife, who like Christ, has always been there for me. My love for my wife, as for Christ, cannot be put into words, but is the language of the soul and heart, and knows no boundaries. My dear wife went to be with Jesus 8/12/13. I dedicate the completion of this book to my Christian wife, Patricia Ann McPeters. How I miss her, and long to be with her, and I most surely will be very soon, (50 years of marriage, and I love you honey).

I am humbled and honored by the endorsement of my pastor and friend, Rev. Johnny Sawyer. He has, by way of example, instilled in me the spirit of humility with perseverance. I have also found Rev. Sawyer to be a man of excellent wisdom. I would like to acknowledge five men of God, who over the years have made an impact on my life:

- Dr. Vernon Truitt
- Rev. Douglas Carver
- Rev. David Gunter
- Rev. Johnny Sawyer
- Rev. James (Tommy) Stewart

Because of the controversy, and the contradictions of views of the interpretations of the book Revelation, I have decided to stand alone in my convictions and views of this book. Also Rev. Joseph Small, who help make it possible to get this book printed, a true friend. I would also like to thank a good friend, William "Tommy" Phillips for his assistance in the typing of this book. My thanks goes out to Mr. Bernard (Bernie) Easler for his help in connecting me with Create Space Publishing. Bernie has been a true blessing, and a good friend. Mr. Bernard is well known in the arena of gospel music. I would also like thank David Hendricks for his assistance. A special thanks to my great niece, Sonya Aguilar, for the final editing and formatting of this book. Last but not least, I would like to thank my nephew, Weldon James for the cover picture.

Dear Reader,

Please give me the courtesy that you would expect to receive from me if you desired to share something of interest with me. Hear me through then by all means and for truth's sake, judge the words and thoughts that I express throughout this book. The Bible tells us to prove all things (II Corinthians 13:1). Compare scripture with scripture. Letting the Bible be its own interpreter. After all has been said, God's word is the final authority. After following this safe and scriptural rule, let everyone be fully persuaded in his own mind. We must all answer to God and give an account for every word that parts our lips.

BOOK ENDORSEMENT

The rarity of an item is often what gives it great value. When the U. S. Treasury Department mints coins with anomalies and a few accidentally find their way into circulation, those rare coins become very valuable. Other items of rarity and great worth, such as gold, silver, and diamonds, are lying undiscovered, hidden in dark, deep places. Only after long and arduous seeking can someone exclaim, "Eureka! I have found it!"

You are about to enter a study and you will often hear yourself saying, "I get it now!" This is because Rev. Gerald McPeters has spent a lifetime of study and discovery as he searched and discovered the hidden treasures of the book of Revelation. Rev. McPeters has uncovered these deep spiritual truths and made them very accessible for the followers of Jesus.

These discoveries were not made in a closed off academic setting but in the frontline trenches of the church engaged in spiritual warfare. Rev. McPeters has spent countless hours shutting himself off from the deafening voices of this world to seek the heavenly solitude of Divine revelation that is unveiled in God's Holy Word. As these discoveries were made, great effort was made by Gerald to faithfully preach and teach these truths!

As Rev. Gerald McPeter's pastor for the past sixteen years, it is my pleasure to highly recommend "*The Patmos Vision*" for both personal enrichment and corporate Bible Study. The Riches you will discover come from the heart of a Bible student, and from a holy heart. This man loves God!

Rev. Johnny R. Sawyer, M.Div.
Lead Pastor
Ranlo Church of God
www.ranlochurchofgod.com

CONTENTS

INTRODUCTION

I will cover all 22 chapters in the book Revelation briefly only to guide the reader. The challenge of understanding the book of Revelation is to interpret the many symbols, types, shadows, metaphors, figurative language, the law of double reference, and the parenthetical scriptures .The book Revelation is in chronological order. There are many parenthetical scriptures, verses, and chapters. Knowledge of this is very important as you seek to have a better understanding of this prophecy. Also, it would be most wise never be dogmatic in our interpretation of this prophecy. This is a study book, not another bible. Let God be true, and every man a liar.

This revelation was given to John around 96 A. D. at the time of this revelation the Church was undergoing persecution by the Roman Emperors. The Apostle John was the last of the Twelve Apostles, and was at this time the *"District Overseer"* of the seven churches of Asia Minor, or so it would seem. This vision was given in reference to the Day of the Lord (yet future). Five witnesses prove the authenticity of the revelation: God the Father, God the Son, the Messenger Angel, the Holy Spirit, and of course John.

This is a book of revelations, not mysteries. This is an open book to be clearly understood by the church. The very title of the book puts aside all mysterious misgivings. The word revelation defined, is to uncover, unveil, bring to surface, to make visible, and bring to light the things which were once mysteries. The *chief theme* of Revelation is to bring Israel into covenant with Jesus Christ, and the tribulation.

John was banished to Patmos because of the preaching of God's word and his testimony of Jesus Christ. On the first day of the week, being the Lord's Day *Sunday*, while John was in prayer under the Anointing of the *"Holy Ghost"*. God spoke to him in a very loud voice, as of a trumpet. As

John was turning to see the voice that spoke unto him, he had envisioned the revelation of Jesus Christ. As this revelation unfolds before his eyes, he looked into the past, present, and future of Christ's Church.

There is a promise to all who hear and keep the prophecy of this book. There are only two mysteries in this book: The voice of the seven thunders and the half hour of silence. These mysteries will unfold in God's own time.

Concerning this prophecy, it was of old given in the days of Daniel the prophet; however, Daniel was told to seal up the prophecy until the end of the time. Therefore, this prophecy was a mystery in the days of Daniel. (Daniel 12:4, 9-10)However we are not living in Daniel's day but rather the last days. Jesus has broken the seals that Daniel sealed the book of prophecy with. (Revelation 5:1-7, 6:1-2, 8:1) Therefore, the prophecy is no longer a mystery, but now a revelation. Thus, the very title of the book shows it to be a book of revelations.

For those of you who feel that this revelation does not concern the church, then why is it addressed to the churches? For those of you who feel that this should be left alone and unread, then what of the promise of blessing to the ones who read and hear this prophecy? (Revelation1:3) The church is to warn the world of coming judgment as Noah of old. Jesus is the author, John is the writer. This is the same John that Jesus left his mother with, the youngest of twelve apostles, and the last of the 12 apostles. We have no record of John's death. Think about that!

The extent of this study is to explore the signs of Christ's Return and tribulation. The big question is, when shall these things be, and what shall be the sign of thy coming? The answer is found in scripture. (Matthew 24:36 & Matthew 24:44)

Prophecy is being fulfilled every day. It is possible we are now in the beginning of sorrows. (Matthew 24:8) The United States of America is turning away from God and turning against Israel: President Obama stated on National News, "we are no longer just a Christian Nation" and now promotes gay marriage in direct defiance of God's word.

Are you saved, have you been born again? Are you really ready for the coming of the Lord, or maybe the fall of America, when the Church could go underground?

THE SINNER'S PRAYER

Father God, I come as I am, and ask you Holy Father to forgive me for all my sins for Jesus' sake and come into my heart and be my lord, now and forever. I truly believe Jesus is your son, and He was born of the Virgin Mary: and died for my sin, and rose again for my salvation. Amen

GLOBAL COMMUNITY

SPREAD THE WEALTH

Webster's definition of community is "mutual participation: a society of persons under the same law". Ever hear of Community Organizer? I had to say it.

"And all that dwell upon the earth shall worship him." (Revelation 13:8) (Antichrist)

"And it was given unto him to make war with the saints and to overcome them: and power was given unto him over all kindred, and tongues, and nations." (Revelation 13:7)

I am of the opinion and have been for years that the New Age Movement is the curtain that will reveal the Antichrist and usher in the *"New World Order"* controlled by the United Nations with one world government.

Is it possible that the little community organizer could be the little horn of Daniel 7: 8. I do not think so, but what a thought. He is of the spirit of the Antichrist, as are all who reject Jesus Christ as the *"only"* means of salvation.

President Obama just got re-elected for a second term. The home of the brave and the land of the free have fallen and great is that fall. Can America survive four more years? What will Israel do now without the full support of America? Some say they will do what they have to do alone; however, God will as always go with them. Who will stand with America? If America forsakes Israel, God will forsake America. Then what?

"And I will bless them that bless thee, and curse him that curseth thee." (Genesis 12: 3)

"And the wicked shall be turned into hell, and all nations that forgot God." (Psalms 19: 17)

CHAPTER ONE OUTLINE

- ❖ The Revelation of Jesus Christ

- ❖ The first begotten

- ❖ The Faithful Witness

- ❖ The Priestly Robe

- ❖ The Golden Girdle

- ❖ His Feet, Eyes, and Hair

- ❖ The Two-Edged Sword

- ❖ The Face of Christ (God)

- ❖ The Seven Churches, the Seven Candlesticks, the Seven Pastors, the Seven Stars, and the Seven Angels

- ❖ The Three Divisions of the Book

- ❖ A Promise of a Blessing to anyone who would read or hear the words of this prophecy (Revelation 1:3)

CHAPTER ONE

Jesus Christ Portrayed as High Priest of the New Covenant

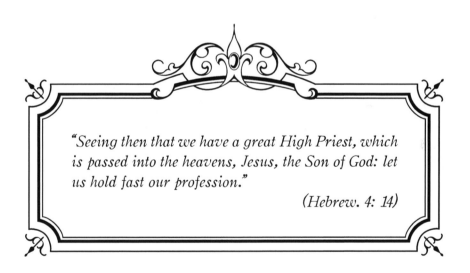

"Seeing then that we have a great High Priest, which is passed into the heavens, Jesus, the Son of God: let us hold fast our profession."

(Hebrew. 4: 14)

Chapter one opens with the Revelation of Jesus Christ in his glory and in the power of his resurrection. In this chapter, Jesus Christ is the first begotten from the dead, meaning, the first fruits of the first resurrection or the first man born of woman to be changed, or quickened and bodily raptured to heaven. (Matthew 27:52-53). Many graves opened and, many dead bodies arose. (Ephesians 4:8-10) The many that arose from the graves also were raptured with Jesus. Jesus is called the faithful witness, in that he was unto death without sin. He is the Prince of the Kings of the earth, and greater than the greatest. Most of all, Jesus is the one who washed us from our sins with the blood he shed on the old rugged cross. John gives this description of Jesus Christ in the vision:

Jesus is dressed in his priestly robe to fill his office as high priest of the New Testament. His head and hairs were white as wool, which symbolizes wisdom and holiness. He wore a golden girdle as a symbol of victory. His feet were as fine brass, which symbolized Jesus had passed through the fires of the trials of life. His eyes were as a flame of fire, which symbolized his power to detect the thoughts and intents of the heart. His voice was as the sound of many waters, the voice of God as water reaching out to many people. The sharp two edged sword, which is the word of God, cuts both ways. His face portrays the full glory of God as the sun in full strength. Jesus is the Alpha and the Omega: the beginning and the end, the first and the last. (Revelation 1: 12-16).

After the vision of Christ, John is commanded to write in a book the vision and to send the book to the seven churches of Asia which are symbolized by the seven candlesticks, and the pastors which are symbolized by the seven stars and the seven angels.

John is told to write the things which thou hast seen, the things which are, and the things which shall be hereafter: therefore, this book has three divisions: past, present, and future. There is a Promise of a blessing to all who read or hears the words of this Prophecy. (Revelation 1:3)

ADDITIONAL EXPLANATORY NOTES

"And the graves were opened, and many bodies of the saints which slept arose and came out of the graves after his resurrection and went into the Holy City, and appeared unto many." (Matthew 27: 52-53)

"JESUS AS HIGH PRIEST"

"Seeing then that we have a great High Priest, which is passed into the heavens, Jesus, the Son of God: let us hold fast our profession." (Hebrew. 4: 14)

The High Priest is the one who offers sacrifice for the sins of the people once a year as he would enter the Holy of Holies. However, Jesus became our high priest by offering up himself, *once and for all*. He that knew no sin became sin. Jesus Christ became *"The Sin Offering."*

"Behold the Lamb, (Sacrifice) of God, which taketh away the sin of the world. Again, Verse 36 and looking up on Jesus as he walked, he saith, behold the Lamb of God." (St. John 1:29).

"Behold he comes with clouds". (Revelation 1:7) The "clouds" represents *all* the saints of all ages including the church that was raptured in Revelation 4:1. This is speaking of the second coming, when everyone will see him, also the ones who pierced him. We also see in Hebrew 12:1, a great cloud of witnesses that will be part of his second coming. (Revelation 19).

It is worthy to note, that Jesus holds the church in his right hand, as is represented by the seven stars. (Revelation 1: 20) Seven is God's number for one, (whole 7 = 1) with God. No man can pluck the church out of his hand, as long as we stay faithful.

JESUS IS THE SEED OF THE WOMAN

"And I will put enmity (difference) between thee and the woman and between thy seed, and her seed, (Christ) it shall bruise your head, and thou (Jesus Christ) shall bruise his heel." (Genesis 3: 15)

"But when the fullness of time was come, God Sent forth his son made of a woman (Mary) made under the law." (Galatians. 4: 4)

"Remember that Jesus Christ of the seed of David was raised from the dead, according to my Gospel." (II Timothy. 2: 8)

"For verily he took not on him the nature of angels: but he took on him the seed of Abraham." (Hebrew. 2:16)

Mary being of the seed (linage) of Abraham provided Jesus a human body of flesh and bone. Yet, no Adamic blood flowed through his veins, as he was conceived by the Holy Ghost (God). (Mat. 1: 20-21à "The God Man").

"He is the Lion of the tribe of Judah, the root of David being the seed (Christ) of the woman" (Mary), Gen. 3:15. (Isaiah 7: 14, Matthew 1: 18-23: Luke 1: 34).

"But when the fullness of time was come, God sent forth his son, made of a woman (Mary), made under the law to redeem them who were under the law." (Galatians. 4:4)

"And again Isaiah said, there shall be a "root" of Jesses, (Jesus Christ), and he shall rise to reign over the Gentiles." (Romans 15: 12) This concerns Jesus coming from the family of King David according to the flesh, as Mary provided that Human body, Mary being of the family of King David." Jesus the God Man is 100% God and 100% man.

CHAPTER TWO OUTLINE

❖ Again, the Seven Churches

❖ God's Number seven

❖ Ephesus, Smyrna, Pergamos, Thyatira, Sardis, Philadelphia, and Laodicea

❖ 7 = One Whole or One Church Age or Dispensation

❖ Discuss the Condition of Each Church and the way God sees his Church

CHAPTER TWO

The Seven Churches

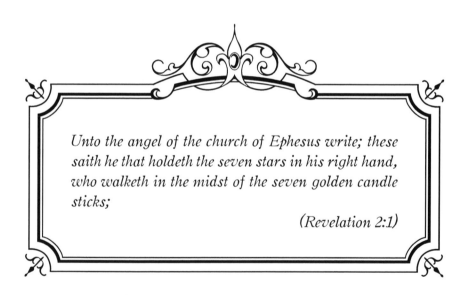

Unto the angel of the church of Ephesus write; these saith he that holdeth the seven stars in his right hand, who walketh in the midst of the seven golden candle sticks;

(Revelation 2:1)

John writes the things which are the seven churches (church age). Remember God's number seven represents a whole, or the one church. God's number for a whole is seven in the book Revelation, seven churches, seven spirits, seven candlesticks, seven angels, seven seals, seven trumpets, seven vials, seven stars, seven lamps of fire, seven horns, seven eyes of Jesus, seven heads, seven thunders, seven thousand men, seven months, seven plagues, seven mountains, and seven kings. A minority out of all seven churches or seven ages or time periods, will make up the one church. (In all seven churches you can see today's church.) The Luke warmness, loss of first love, hypocrites, weak in faith, dead service, rich in finances and members but poor in their faith, compromising, yet still holding on to the name of Jesus Christ. (There are many good churches which are true to the Lord.)

The Bible says, "whosoever nameth the name of Christ, let him depart from sin." In the midst of today's church, you will find the true church (faithful few). All had to repent and do their works over. When the Rapture takes place, it will be a day of separation where the tares will be separated from the wheat. (Revelation 4:1) The church will be separated from the false church.

I will not go into the seven phases of Church History, beginning with Christ. (The New Testament until the Rapture) I will only say that a number of all seven churches, or seven ages, will make up the one church that will be raptured up. (Corinthians 15:51-52) The true church is not any one organization, but rather *"Body of Christ"*. The true church will be the called out ones, or the Raptured ones. We will see later, the rapture of the church is pictured in Revelations 4:1.

Ephesus (desired newly born): This church is believed to be the beginning of the apostolic church. The Church of Ephesus was strict in this sense. They did not tolerate sin among their members, nor did they take into their fellowship the uncircumcised, spiritually speaking (the unsaved). Though their standards were high, they grew cold in their own experiences, and they were in need of repentance. Seeing this condition, the Lord commanded that they repent of their self-righteousness and do their first works over. This church was also guilty of the doctrines of the overlords. At this point God demanded repentance or he would destroy the church.

Smyrna-Myrth: The church of Smyrna was found without fault in the eyes of the Lord. They were poor in material things, yet rich with faith in God. There was a time of persecution in the lives of those Christians, yet they greatly matured in the faith because of trying times. *"Think it not strange concerning fiery trails..." (I Peter 4:12).*

Pergamos (worldly): The church of Pergamos was located in a place where the gospel of Christ was not well known, the place was known as Satan's seat, for example would be China. The Pergamos church held the doctrine of Balaam, which is a doctrine of compromising. (Numbers 22:24, 31:16) Just as Balaam compromised and betrayed Israel to have favor with the king, just as the church compromise the gospel to have favor with the world. Mega Churches with great surplus are not necessarily a sign of God's Blessing. When anything is taken into the church it belittles the church, and a little leaven will spoil the whole. What will the organized church do now as the Federal Government says we must offer membership to homosexuals? Will the organized church go the way of Balaam? Yes it surely will: or surely has. President Obama now supports gay marriage, can you believe this? He says that America is no longer a Christian nation, well, while it is true we have become a cage of every unclean and hateful bird, in other words, false religions. (Rev, 18: 2) Yet, we are still a Christian nation.

Thyatira (works of faith and sacrifice): The church of Thyatira was growing in love and works of faith in Christ. The minority, however, held the doctrine of Jezebel, which is simply worldliness, pretense, and compromising. An example would be modern day Pentecostals that are conforming to the fads of this age, thus bringing reproach to the holiness people. This group is in desperate need of repentance. (These are the Hollywood Pentecostals).

CHAPTER THREE OUTLINE

❖ Sardis, Called Out Ones

❖ The Model Church

❖ A lively Church

❖ The Overcomers

❖ The Worthy Ones

CHAPTER THREE

The Overcomers

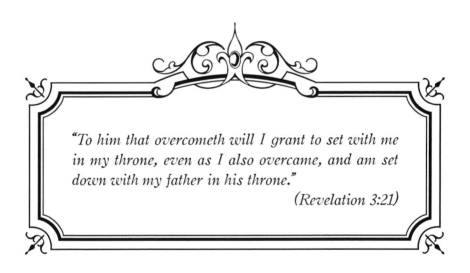

"To him that overcometh will I grant to set with me in my throne, even as I also overcame, and am set down with my father in his throne."

(*Revelation 3:21*)

Sardis (called out ones): The church of Sardis, according to the scriptures, had an evangelistic outreach in the sense, it was highly spoken of throughout the land and was looked upon as a lively church, "Thou hast a name that thou livest and art dead" (Revelation 3: 1). Man accepted Sardis as a model church of that day; however, God looked upon it as a church that was not sensitive to the needs of the people because of their desire to make a name for themselves. They were growing in numbers, yet, were spiritually dead.

Philadelphia, (brotherly love): The Church of Philadelphia had an open door in the sense that they could witness without persecution of any great degree. They were free to worship as they chose, because many people of that district were believers in Christ, yet they were weak because there was no persecution to keep them on their knees. Great faith is a result of great battles and much sacrifice.

Laodicea (the people rule). The church of Laodicea had become lukewarm in their experience, active in the work of the church, but no prayer life, no burden for the lost. They were very prosperous in material goods, yet God said that they were poor, naked, blind, miserable, and in great need of repentance. In this church we see Jesus standing on the outside trying to enter. Will anyone hear what the spirit said to the churches?

There will be the Rapture of the church (Revelation 4:1). Then the last seven years that follows the Rapture is the Seven Year Tribulation, or the 70th week as referenced in Daniel 9:27. This placed the church age between the 69th and 70th week of Daniel 9: 27. This is referred to as the "Gap Theory".

"And he, (Antichrist) shall confirm the covenant with many for one week (or seven years), and in the midst of the week, he shall cause the sacrifice and the *oblations to cease." (Daniel 9: 27)* In the middle of the seven years will be the time of *"Jacob's Trouble"* (Jeremiah 30:7), and is known as the *"Great Tribulation."*

The Antichrist is called the *"Prince of the Covenant"* (Daniel 11:21-23) *"And in his estate shall stand a vile person, to whom they shall not give the honour of the kingdom he shall come in peaceably and obtain the kingdom by flatteries. And with the arms of a flood shall they be overthrown from before him, and shall be broken: yea, also the prince of covenant"* (Daniel

11:21-23) He shall confirm the covenant with many for *one week*. "*The Great Tribulation*" of course is "*Jacob's Trouble*" which will be the last three and a half years as referenced in Jeramiah30:7.

"*Alas, for that day is great, so that none is like it: it is even the time of Jacob's trouble, but he shall be saved out of it.*" (Jeremiah 30: 7)

"*And he shall speak great words against the most high, and shall wear out the saints of the most high, and think to change times and laws and they shall be given into his hands until a time and times and the dividing of times.*" (Daniel 7:25)

"*And at that time shall Michael stand up, the great prince which standeth for the children of thy people: And there shall be a time of trouble, such as never was since there was a nation even to that same time: and at that time thy people shall be delivered, everyone that shall be found written In the book*" (Daniel 12:1)

"*But the court which is without the temple leave out, and measure it not: for it is given unto the Gentiles: and the holy city shall they tread under foot forty and two months*" (Revelations 11:2)

"*And the woman fled into the wilderness, where she hath a place prepared of God that they should feed her there a thousand two hundred and threescore days.*" (Revelations12:6)

"*And to the woman were given two wings of a great eagle, which she might fly into the wilderness, into her place, where she is nourished for a time, and times, and half a time, from the face of the Serpent.*" (Revelations 12:14)

ADDITIONAL EXPLANATORY NOTES

The Ephesus time period represented from the calling of the 12 Apostles until John who was, the last of the 12 Apostles. In fact, this prophecy or book revelation was written around 96 A. D. and is believe that St. John died shortly after receiving this revelation; however, we know nothing of his death, other than what tradition tell us. (The writings of Irenaeus) Even though other great men followed, such as John's disciple, an example Polycarp, the 12 apostles will never be replaced. No record of John's death presents the possibility that John could be one of the two prophets in Revelation 11: Remember the words of Jesus to Peter "what is that to you if he is here when I return?"(John 21:22)

The church of Smyrna (time period approximately 100 A.D. -300 A.D. was known as the suffering church because of Roman persecution, This church was very poor in materials goods, but very strong in faith.

The church of Pergamos (from 300 A. D. – 500 A. D.) was the first state church, which laid the foundation for the Catholic Church, and the beginning of Catholicism.

The church of Thyatira (500 A. D. till present day) is known as the papal church which was the beginning of Catholicism. However, there were many people in this church who loved Jesus, as is true of many Catholics today, in spite of its false teachings.

The church of Sardis (around 1500 A. D.) is known as the *"Reformation Church"*. It produced many good works, but was weak in faith.

The Philadelphia church (1800 A D) until present day, overlapping the Laodicea church age) is known as the missionary church that would reach the world with the gospel of Jesus Christ.

The Laodicea church (20th Century) is known as today's church

CHAPTER FOUR OUTLINE

❖ Time of Christ's Return

❖ The Open Door

❖ John Caught up

❖ Things Hereafter (Future Events)

❖ The Body of Christ- Church-Jew and Gentiles

❖ The Beginning of the 70th Week, (Daniel 9:27)

❖ Between the 69th and 70th week of Daniel, 70th week is referred to as the *"Gap Theory"* or the Church Age.

CHAPTER FOUR

The Rapture of the Church

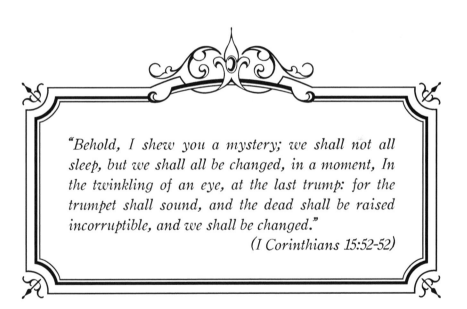

"Behold, I shew you a mystery; we shall not all sleep, but we shall all be changed, in a moment, In the twinkling of an eye, at the last trump: for the trumpet shall sound, and the dead shall be raised incorruptible, and we shall be changed."

(I Corinthians 15:52-52)

"THE OPEN DOOR"

"COME UP HIGHER"

While it is true John was caught up to Heaven, whether in the body or out of the body, we are not sure, this seems to make this a type of the Rapture. For what purpose was John caught up to Heaven? Answer: "I will show thee things which must be here after…" (Revelations 4:1).

I THESSALONIANS 14:13-18

The Thessalonians were confused about the time of the rapture. Some thought the rapture had already come: others thought there were not going to be raptured, and were concerned about their deceased love ones. St. Paul wrote to inform them that the rapture had not come yet, and that they need not worry about their deceased who died in Christ, for that day is yet future. To say the least, I believe we (the Church) will see the Antichrist before we go up, I may be wrong, but we will see soon.

Although the word rapture is not in the bible, there are several words used that signify rapture. These words include but are not limited to: resurrection, redemption, delivered, awake, and mystery. References to the rapture are found in the following scriptures:

Redemption: "and grieve not the Holy Ghost of God, where by ye are sealed unto the day of your redemption." (Ephesians 4:30)

"Even we ourselves groan within ourselves, waiting for the adoption, to wit, the Redemption (Rapture) of our body". (Romans 8:23)

"And when these things begin to come to pass, then look up, and lift up your heads: for your Redemption draweth nigh." (Luke 21:28)

"That I may know him, and the Power of his resurrection, and the fellowship of his sufferings, being made conformable unto his death, if by any means I might attain unto the resurrection of the dead." (Philippians 3: 10-11)

"Women received their dead raised to life again: and others were tortured, not accepting deliverance: that they might obtain a better resurrection." (Hebrews 11:35)

"And thou shalt be blessed: for they cannot recompense thee: for, thou shalt be recompensed at the resurrection of the just." (II Kings 14:14)

TIME OF CHRISTS RETURN

"So likewise ye, when ye shall see all these things, know that it is near, even at the door." (Matthew 24:33)

"But of that day and hour knoweth no man. No! Not the angels of Heaven, but only my Father." (Matthew 24:36)

"Therefore be ye also ready: for in such an hour as ye think not, the son of man cometh." (Matthew 24:44)

THERE ARE FIVE RAPTURES IN SCRIPTURE, BUT THERE WILL BE ONLY ONE CHURCH RAPTURE.

- The *first rapture* is the rapture of Jesus and the bodies who came out of the graves (Matthew 27:52-53)
- The *second rapture* is the rapture of the Church (Revelation 4:1)
- The *third rapture* is the rapture of the two Prophets (Revelation 11:3-12)
- The *fourth rapture* is the rapture where we see 144,000 Jews before God's throne playing their harpers. *"And I looked and lo, a lamb stood on the Mount Sion, and with him an hundred forty and four thousand, having his father's name written in their foreheads. And I heard a voice from heaven, as the voice of many waters, and as the voice of a great thunder: and I heard the voice of harpers harping with their harps. And they sung as it were a new song before the throne and before the four beasts and the elders: and no man could learn that song but the hundred and forty and four thousand, which were redeemed from the earth." (Revelation 14: 1-3)*
- The *fifth rapture* would be the souls *"under the alter"* they were beheaded for their faith in Christ and told to rest yet a little while until their brethren, the mixed multitude as they should be martyred as they were. The fifth rapture with the mixed multitude, *"a great multitude which no man could number, of all nations and kindreds, and people, and tongues, stood before the throne, and before the lamb, clothes with white robes, and palms in their hands; and cried with a loud voice, saying, Salvation to our God which sitteth upon the throne, and unto the lamb. And all the angels stood round about the throne,*

and about the elders and the four beasts, and fell before the throne on their faces and worshipped God. Saying, Amen: Blessing, and glory, and wisdom, and thanksgiving, and honour, and power, and might, be unto our God for ever and ever. Amen. And one of the elders answered, saying unto me, what are these which are arrayed in white ropes? And whence came they? And I said unto him, Sir, thou knowest. And he said to me, these are they which came out of great tribulation, and have washed their robes and made them white in the blood of the lamb." (Revelation 7:9-14) While we do not know when this rapture will take place, we know it was some time near the end of tribulation. *"And what shall be the sign of thy coming, and of the end of the world?" (Matthew 24:3)* Now this would seem to be speaking of the second coming, as most of the signs here take place during the tribulation.

The rapture and the second coming are often confused. Jesus comes first to rapture the church. (Revelation 4: 1) Then seven years later, Christ returns with the church, and every eye shall see him, even those who pierced him. (II Peter 3:10-12). The rapture and the second coming are two different events, not two phases of the same event. When the Bible speaks of the second coming, we should not confuse this with the rapture: there are seven years that separates these two events.

"THE MYSTERY OF GOD"

The mystery of God is the body of Jesus Christ (church) made up of not only natural Jews, but also Gentiles. We are the seed of Abraham, who is the father of all that believe. *"Know ye therefore that they which are of faith, the same are the children of Abraham. And the Scripture, foreseeing that God would justify the heathen (Gentiles) Through faith preached before the gospel unto Abraham, saying in thee shall all nations be blessed .So then they which be of faith are blessed with faithful Abraham."(Galatians3: 7-9)* For the gospel, was first preached unto Abraham and Abraham believed the gospel, and it was counted unto him for righteousness. Abraham knew Jesus Christ very well. He had a personal relationship with Christ. He was saved by faith, and justified by faith, in modern day known as *born again.*

There is only one gospel, and the gospel is the good news which is Jesus Christ, the power of God into salvation.

The word Rapture is not found in God's word, but we understand the word rapture to mean resurrection, (I Corinthians 15:51-52). We will be resurrected at his coming. The rapture is referred to as a mystery in the book Corinthians because Paul was the first to receive the *"Full Revelation"* of this event. Many believed in the resurrection, but no one understood nor did they understand this to be the body of Christ, made up of Jew and Gentile believers. Also, they understood nothing of the living saints being raptured. This was the mystery kept secret from the foundation of the world, and even from the Old Testament prophets.

While most scholars' calls The Falling Away in II Thessalonians 2:3 the *"Great Apostasy"* other scholars say Thessalonians 2:3 verse should be translated, "for that day shall not come except there come a "departure" first": this could give more credence to the Rapture taking place before the beginning of the 70th week or 7 year tribulation. !

The words "falling away" means to fall back or quit, give up, the word "departure" means to leave or be moved, like the Exodus of Egypt, to cross over to the other side. The seventh week equals the seven year covenant, which will be broken in the middle of week. (Daniel 9:27, 11:22-23)

SCRIPTURES THAT REFERENCE TO THE ANTICHRIST

1. "He is a vile person." (Daniel 11:21). "He will come first as a man of peace and will win over many with flatteries."
2. "He is called the Prince of the Covenant." (Daniel 11:22): "which he will break in the middle of the week." (Daniel 9:27)
3. His beginning will be as the Little Horn of Daniel 7:8.
4. "He will be self-willed." (Daniel 11:16).
5. "He will not regard the God of his father."
6. "Appears to be a homosexual in that he has no desire for women." (Daniel 11:39)
7. "He will divide the land." (Daniel 11:39)
8. "He will be a man of fierce countenance (understanding dark or deep mysteries)." (Daniel 8:23)

9. "He will have power to destroy the people of God." (Daniel 8:24: Dan. 7:21,25: Revelation 15:7)

10. "He stops the daily sacrifice." (Daniel 8:12: Daniel 9:27.)

11. "He will be called "Man of Sin". (II Thessalonians 2:3)

12. "He is the "Son of Perdition".

13. "He will be called "That Wicked". (II Thessalonians 2:8)

14. He is the "White Horse Rider" of Revelation 6:2.

15. He is "The Great Red Dragon" of Revelation 12:3.

16. He will be called "The Devil". (Revelation 12:12, 7, 9, 20:10)

17. He will be called "The Beast". (Revelation 12: 1-2, 17:11, 13, 19:19-20)

18. He will be called "The Antichrist" only once. (I John 2:18)

19. He will be called "The Assyrian". (Isaiah 10:20-27)

20. He will be called "King of Babylon". (Isaiah 14:4)

21. He will be called "The Spoiler". (Isaiah 16:4)

22. He will be called "The Extortioner". (Isaiah 16:4)

"EXTENT OF THE GREAT TRIBULATION"

The last three and a half years concern the *"Great Tribulation"*. We see three and a half years many times given in reference to *"Great tribulation"*. The following are scriptures with reference to the "Great Tribulation" (Daniel 7:25: Revelation 11:12: Revelation 12:6. Daniel 9:26-27: Daniel 12:7: Revelation 13:5: Jeremiah 30:7).

We are now seeing the *"New World Order"* unfold before our eyes, with the changing of times and laws as referenced in Daniel 7:25. There is an unprecedented call for a change in the *Constitution of the United States* of America. *"New World Order"* became a household word under the Bush Sr. administration. I believe the true church will go underground in America soon. I hope I am wrong. One thing is for certain, we are not home yet. This seems to agree with II Thessalonian 2:3. Not only does this tell us how long the Tribulation Saints will be under the control of the antichrist (three and half years) It also tells us this tribulation of God's Saints will only end at the coming of the Lord to set up his earthly kingdom.

"Until the Ancient of days came, and judgment was given to the saints

of the most high: and the time came that the saints possessed the kingdom."
(Daniel 7:22)

The Ancient of days is not going to set up his kingdom on earth for his saints to possess, until the end of the tribulation. Then we (the church) will be in control and will rule and reign with Christ. What a day that will be all human governments destroyed.

"ANCIENT OF DAYS"

What happens when the Ancient of Days comes?

First: Thrones (kingdoms) are cast down. All the governments of this earth are cast down, destroyed and the Antichrist as well. (Daniel 7:9)

Second: The books were opened (books of records of the deeds of every man of earth). (Revelation)

Third: The Antichrist is destroyed and given to the burning flame. (Revelation)

Fourth: Christ sets up his kingdom. (Revelation)

Notice the other beasts (kings), lives were prolonged for a season, and time. Now this is not duration of time, but rather a particular set time, given to these other beasts for a purpose unknown, maybe a space to repent, but this is debatable. (Daniel 7:12)

Revelation 20:1-15 speaks of two resurrections, one for the righteous and one for the unrighteous. These seem to be one thousand years apart.

"And at that time shall Michael stand up, the great prince which standeth for the children of thy people (Israel), and there will be a time of trouble such as never was since there was a nation even to that same time? And at that time thy people will be delivered, everyone that shall be found written in the book. And many of them that sleep in the dust of the earth shall awake, some to everlasting life, and some to shame and everlasting contempt." (Daniel 12:1-2)

"Alas! For that day is great, so that none is like it: it is even the time of Jacob's trouble, but he shall be saved out of it." Jeremiah 30:7:

Revelation 20:5 speaks of the rest of the dead lived not again, until the 1000 years had ended. I believe this to mean the converted sinner who survived the tribulation to enter into the millennial to replenish the earth as natural people? Could it be that the second resurrection consist of the left-overs of tribulation that are judged during this 1000 years will be resurrected at the last and final Day of Judgment (White Throne)? Many will come to Christ during this time, but not everyone will receive Christ even then, (Revelation 20:5, 12:-15).

"THE DEAD IN CHRIST"

As referenced in Revelation 6:9-11, not only all who had been beheaded during tribulation, but also, all saints of all ages who had died and gone on to be with the lord, as Jesus is coming with all his saints, not just a set number.

"To the end he may establish your hearts blameless in holiness before God, even our Father, at the coming of our Lord Jesus Christ with all his saints."(I Thessalonians 3:13)

And Enoch also, the seventh from Adam, prophesied of these saying, Behold, the Lord cometh with ten thousands of his saints, (Jude 1:14)

"Again, Jesus is coming with all his saints." (Zechariah 14:1-5)

The first resurrection will consist of the living and the dead saints, not sinners. The converted sinners that make it through tribulation will replenish the earth. These are the people who refuse to take the mark of the antichrist, of every nation under heaven, a mixed multitude. (Not the same as the mixed multitude of Revelation 7: 9-11)

WHEN SHALL THESE THINGS BE?

The question was asked, "When shall these things be, and what shall be the sign of thy coming, (second coming), and of the end of the world?" (Matthew 24:3) While Matthew 24:36 clearly states no man knows the day (very day), or hour when the son of man will come, not even the angels. Yet Jesus did say in Matthew 24:33, that when ye see these things come to pass, look up for your Redemption is near. (Rapture of the Body) What *"things "* is Jesus speaking of? Jesus gave us certain signs to tell us or show that it is near time of his return.(Matthew 24:7-8) Wars, earthquakes, famine, hunger, but the greatest sign was given in Matthew 24:29-31 *"Immediately after the tribulation of those days, shall the sun be darkened, and the moon shall not give her light, and the stars shall fall from heaven, and the powers of the heavens shall be shaken: And then shall appear the sign of the son on man in heaven: and then shall all the tribes of earth mourn, and they shall see the son of man coming in the clouds of heaven with power and great glory, and he shall send his angels with a great sound of a trumpet, and they shall gather together his elect (saints) from the four winds, from one end of heaven to the other."* The greatest sign of his second coming as referenced in Revelation 19: 11-14 are the signs of tribulation as referenced in Matthew 24:8.24:34-44. Again, Matthew 24:36 tells us no man knows the day or the hour of his coming, (rapture or second coming) but my brother, when the sun becomes black and the moon is as blood, and the antichrist begins to put Gods saints to death, then you can be sure his second coming is near.

Some teach that the rapture must take place before the antichrist is revealed. As referenced in II Thessalonians 2:7-8, they say the *"He"* who now letteth that is to be taken out of the way is the church, and then after the church is taken out of the way the wicked one will be revealed. II Thessalonians 2:3 tells us that this day of gathering in rapture shall not come until the man of sin is first revealed. I believe the church will see the Antichrist before we are raptured, but that is debatable.

He (the church) will be out of the way, making an easy way for Antichrist, with his *"new world backers"*.

"THE DAY OF WRATH"

Is God's wrath the same as his judgment? This is the *"Day of Judgment"*. It is when God will pour out his judgments on an unbelieving Christ rejecting world. I believe *""Mystery Babylon""*, to be America, and the *"beast"* to be the antichrist. The woman (Rome) carried the antichrist as the false prophet whom I believe to be the pope. *"And I beheld another beast coming up out of the earth: And he had two horns like a lamb, and he spake as a dragon. And he exercised all the power of the first beast before him, and caused the earth, and them which dwell therein to worship the first beast, who's deadly wound was healed." (Revelation 12:11)*

I must question the true identity of *"Mystery of Babylon"*. The beast is antichrist, the woman the Roman church, *"Mystery Babylon"* and that great city that sitteth upon many waters. I believe the law of double reference must apply as this represents *Rome* as well as *New York City*. This is the same woman in Revelation 17:3 and the harlot of Revelation 17:1. The kings of the earth have committed spiritual fornication with *"Mystery Babylon"* *"New Age"* on her forehead. I must say, New York City comes to mind as part of this mystery. (Revelation 17:2)

George Britt states in his book titled, *"The Hour has come"*, that the one world church will be the union of Catholicism and Protestism as the Emerging *"One World Church of Rome"* the Pope of Rome Calls for Protestant Brothers to come back home to the mother church. Twisting scriptures like in John 17:22, where Jesus prayed *"Father I Pray they be one, even as we are one"*. *(John 17:22)* Will this merge take place? YES INDEED! It is already in the works. This seems to be the clearer picture of *"Mystery Babylon"* as America and Europe are puppets of this woman (Rome) until the new emperor of Europe (the Beast) has no more need of them or her (Revelation 17:1-3, Rev. 17:16-17)

Others say, another possible *One World Order Religion* could and may be *"Chrislam"* making possible that the antichrist could be Muslim. Some, are promoting the merge of Christianity and Islam to be known as chrislam, the list goes on, a high percentage of evangelicals now say, Jesus is not the only way to heaven. Rome, as well as America, has become a cage of every unclean bird (demon), a habitation or place or refuge for all false religions, which really seem to picture America more so than Rome, and unknown wealth, all other nations bow to her, (Rome/America). The President stated on national television, *we are no longer a Christian Nation.*

"Yea, and all that will live godly in Christ Jesus shall suffer persecution." *(II Timothy 3:12)* The world loves its own. Is the servant greater than his Lord, or has persecution come to an end? Are we better than our forefathers? I encourage everyone to read *"Foxes' Book of Martyrs"*. Let us all pray to be worthy to make the rapture.

The seventieth week concerns mostly the Jews; however' tribulation will be world wide in scope. Now with that being said, one must realize that Daniel was praying and seeking to know what would befall his people in the last days. God revealed to him 490 years, in Daniel 9: 24, that were set apart concerning the nation of Israel; however, this did not mean God was not concerned about the rest of mankind during these 490 years. Daniel only ask what would befall his people, after all, Daniel had no understanding of the church. The church was yet a mystery in his day. The ultimate act of crucifixion put an end to sin, finished transgression, and fulfilled prophesy. Jesus became God's *sin offering* to put away sin once for all time. (Hebrew 9:26, John 1:29) Reconciliation for iniquity or to make atonement for sin was accomplished on the cross. (Romans 5:8-12*). "And to seal up the vision and the prophecy." (Romans 10:2-4) "To anoint the most holy." (Daniel 9:24)* The holy of Holies now is the new temple under the new covenant, which is the Body of Christ. This, of course, took place at Pentecost, fifty days after the resurrection of Jesus Christ. The *"Holy of Holies"* under the old covenant became null and void. Some say, it will be the newly Build Temple in Jerusalem, this may be where the *"Law of double Reference"* comes to play. In my opinion it also represents the *"Body of Christ"*. *"What? Know ye not that your body is the temple of the Holy Ghost which is in you, which ye have of God, and ye are not your own."(I Corinthians 6:19)*

"And he (Antichrist) shall confirm the covenant with many for one week he (Antichrist) shall cause the sacrifice and the oblation to cease, and for the over spreading of abomination he shall make it desolate even until the consummation and the determined shall be poured upon the desolate." (Daniel 9: 26-27)

There will be a seven year contract between Israel and antichrist as referenced Daniel 11:21-23. The antichrist is referred to as the *"Prince of the Covenant"* according to Daniel 11:23-24. Never the less, The *"Great Tribulation"* will last three and a half years because the peace treaty is broken in the middle of the week. This will be the time of *"Jacobs Trouble"* (Jeremiah 30:7).

He (the antichrist) will overcome and put to death many tribulation saints for three and a half years. The three and half year are referenced in the following scriptures: Daniel 7:25, 8:14, 12:7, 11, Revelation 12:6, 11:3, 13:5

The seventieth week concerns the Jews only. Now, one must realize that Daniel was praying and seeking to know what would befall his people in the last days. God revealed to him 490 years, in Daniel 9: 24 that were set apart concerning the nation of Israel. This did **not** mean God was not concerned about the rest of mankind during these 490 years. Daniel asked only what would befall his people. After all, Daniel had no understanding of the church. The church was yet a mystery in his day.

NOTE OF INTREST

Please reference the scriptures below out of the **Old Testament** concerning the rapture. Even these men believed in a resurrection of their bodies.

"Thy dead men shall live together with my dead body. They shall arise, awake, and sing, ye that dwell in the dust." (Isaiah. 26:16).

"If a man die, shall he live again. All the days of my appointed time will wait till my change comes." (Job 14:14)

"For I know that my redeemer liveth, and that he shall stand at the latter day upon the earth: and though after my skin worms destroy this body, yet in my flesh shall I see God." (Job 19: 25-26)

"As for me, I will behold thy face in righteousness: I shall be satisfied, when I awake with." (Psalms 17:15)

"Thou, which hast shown me great and sore troubles, shall quicken me again, and shall bring me up again from the depths of the earth." (Psalms71:20)

CHAPTER FIVE OUTLINE

❖ The book with seven seals

❖ One found worthy

❖ The strong Angel.

❖ Angels, Beast, and 24 elders

❖ The Lamb that was slain became the lion of the tribe of Juda

CHAPTER FIVE

"The Book with Seven Seals"

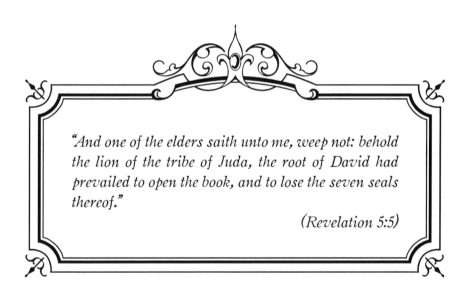

"And one of the elders saith unto me, weep not: behold the lion of the tribe of Juda, the root of David had prevailed to open the book, and to lose the seven seals thereof."

(Revelation 5:5)

John had been caught up to heaven. (Whether he was in the body, or out of body, no one knew) He was taken up to heaven to witness things to come.

"WHO IS WORTHY"

No man was found worthy to open the book and loose the seals or to even look thereon in all heaven and earth, except Jesus. The reason being is because it is the book of the day of judgments and contains the wrath of God that is to be poured out on an unbelieving world of "God-Haters". God is now about to avenge the cry of his people, even the souls under the altar of sacrifice.

Have you ever wondered how it would be and where we would be if no one had been found worthy to break the seals and open the Book? Satan would still be in control doing his thing. All heaven and earth were searched, but no one including the first Adam, Abraham, Moses, the Prophets nor any of the 12 Apostles were found worthy, but there stood a Lamb in the midst of the throne, a Lion of the tribe of Juda, who had become worthy through the offering up of himself for the sins of his people. One of the four and twenty elders fell down and worshipped the Lamb that was slain to redeem them by the shedding of his blood. They sang a new song, "Thou Art Worthy", the angels joined in, ten thousand and thousands of thousands sang unto the lamb, saying worthy is the lamb to receive power, honor, glory, riches, wisdom, strength, and blessing, then all God's creatures on earth and under the earth joined in this new song. The 24 Elders are most likely the 12 major prophets of the Old Testament and the 12 Apostles of the New Testament.

ADDITIONAL NOTES

We see again, two persons of the Trinity of the God Head together at the same time and at the same place. *"And he came and took the book out of the right hand of Him that sat upon the throne." (Revelation 5:7) "I saw in the night vision, and, behold, one like the Son of man (Jesus) came with the clouds of heaven, and came to the Ancient of days (God the Father) and they brought him (Jesus) near before him (God the Father). And there was given him (Jesus) dominion, and glory, and a kingdom, that all people, nations, and Languages, should serve him. (Jesus) his dominion is an everlasting dominion which shall not pass away, and his kingdom that which shall not be destroyed."* (Daniel 7:13) Again, we see the Father and Son together at the same time and same place. This is the book with seven seals that Daniel was told not to break the seals. *"And He said, go thy way, Daniel, for the words are closed up and sealed, till the time of the end." (Daniel 12:9).* It was a mystery in Daniel's time, now it is the *revelation*.

CHAPTER SIX OUTLINE

❖ The first seal broken Daniel 9:27

❖ Beginning of the tribulation-70th wk.

❖ The white horse rider

❖ The red horse rider

❖ The black horse rider

❖ The pale horse rider

❖ Gods' wrath

It is my opinion, this prophecy as a whole is in chronological order, although many parenthetical statements or scriptures often break in that do not fit the present subject. We must rightly divide the word of God, to rightly understand the word of God.

CHAPTER SIX

The Beginning of Tribulation

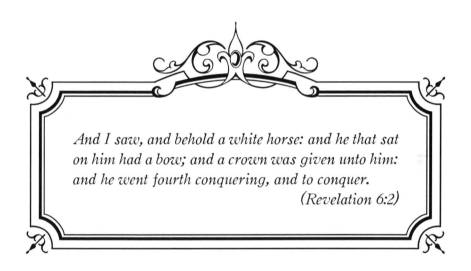

And I saw, and behold a white horse: and he that sat on him had a bow; and a crown was given unto him: and he went fourth conquering, and to conquer.

(Revelation 6:2)

This chapter is the beginning of the seven years of tribulation, known as the 70th week of Daniel 9: 27, and will bring the completion of the 490 years that concerned the Jews, and the *"Holy City"* as referenced in Daniel 9: 21-24. 70 X 70 equals 490 years. Around this time the Antichrist sign a seven year peace treaty with Israel. (Daniel 9:27) The *"White Horse Rider"* will be a man of war, he starts by taking peace from the earth and defeats three countries, Egypt, Libyan, Ethiopians (Daniel 11:43) *"But he shall have power over the treasures of gold and of silver, and over all the precious things of Egypt: and the Libyans and the Ethiopians shall be at his steps" "And of the ten horns that were in his head, and of the other which came up, and before whom three fell, even of that horn that had eyes, and a mouth that spake very great things,whose look was more stout than his fellows".* (Daniel 7:20) *"Alas for that day is great, so that none is like it: it is even the time of Jacob's Trouble: but he shall be saved out of it"* (Jerimiah 30:7) *"Come, my people, enter thou into thy chambers (Petra), and shut thy doors about thee: hide thyself as it were for a little moment, (31/2 year's) until the indignation (tribulation) be over past."* (Isaiah 26:20) The Rock City Petra is in the land of Edom, Moab, these two countries will escape the Antichrist. The Antichrist will be loved and worshipped at his beginning. He will have all the answers and be able to solve complex problems. He will also understand dark sentences. (Daniel 8: 23). From the start, he will go into a seven year contract with Israel which will guarantee peace. (Daniel 9: 27). *"But, by peace will destroy many."*(Daniel 11:22) *"He will be self-willed."* (Daniel 8: 25) *"He will win many over with flatteries."* (Daniel 11: 16) Then in the middle of the tribulation, he will show his hand by breaking his covenant with Israel by putting to death the holy people (Jews) (Daniel 11: 33). He will divide the land for gain is this not what is happening right now. (Daniel11:39).This will be the beginning of Jacobs Trouble, the last 3 ½ years of tribulation.

The purpose of the tribulation is to bring Israel back to their God, according to Matthew 25:32. This chapter opens with six seals. The First Seal is the Rise of the Antichrist out of the Nations of Revived Roman Empire as the little horn spoke in Daniel 7:7, 8. This little horn also represents the revived *"Grecian Empire"* of which the antichrist will be king over. Remember there are ten kingdoms and ten kings. The Antichrist is the Little Horn. The Antichrist will conquer three of the nations. The other kingdoms will surrender their kingdom to Antichrist for one hour. (Revelation 17:12, 13). The Antichrist will be king over the ten nations.

"And it was given unto him to make war with the saints (Israel) and to overcome them: and the power was given him over the whole world kindred's, and tongues, and nations." (Revelation 12:7).

FIRST SEAL

Scriptures references on the Rise of the Antichrist, (Daniel 7:7, 8: 19-25: 8: 8, 9: 20-25, 9:24: 11:35-45)

SECOND SEAL

War follows the *"White Horse Rider",* not peace, again the *White Horse Rider"* is the antichrist here, don't confuse this *"White Horse Rider"* with *"White Horse Rider"* in Revelation 19: which is *"Jesus Christ".*

THIRD SEAL

War brings famine, because of the war in the second seal.

FOURTH SEAL

The fourth seal brings death because of war and lack of food.

FIFTH SEAL

Saints who will not conform to the teachings of the false church, and the *"New World Order"* will be martyred or beheaded, Muslim style. Will the Antichrist be a Muslim? (Revelation 6:9-11, Revelation 7: 13-140)

SIXTH SEAL

A great earthquake takes place. The *"White Horse Rider"* comes talking of peace, and yet he brings along his bow, weapons of war, and war follows him and also death, famine, and hell.

CHAPTER SEVEN OUTLINE

- ❖ The Four Angels

- ❖ The Eastern Angel

- ❖ 144,000 Jews

- ❖ The 12 Tribes of Israel

- ❖ The Great Multitude

- ❖ God's Throne

- ❖ The Elders

- ❖ White Robes

- ❖ Tribulation Saints

CHAPTER SEVEN

The Great Multitude

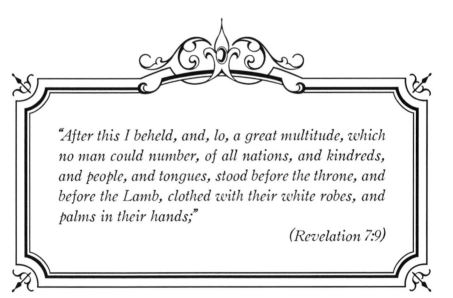

"After this I beheld, and, lo, a great multitude, which no man could number, of all nations, and kindreds, and people, and tongues, stood before the throne, and before the Lamb, clothed with their white robes, and palms in their hands;"

(Revelation 7:9)

We see the *"Throne of God"* surround by Angels, and the Lamb. There will also be a great number of people that have come through, the *"Great Tribulation"* without taking the mark of the beast. Many converted before the millennium but not all. A number of unconverted people will enter the millennium and we, the church, will rule over them. Why is it that the *"White Throne Judgment"* takes place at the end of the 1000 years, and who is to be judged at the *"White Throne"*? The question comes up, why is death destroyed at the end of the 1,000 years? Death is destroyed because sin or the adamic nature is still present during the millennial. There are four angels that are at the four corners of the earth controlling the winds of tribulation for a set time until God says it is time. The *"Eastern Angel"* is to watch over Israel during Israel's restoration. Making these scriptures parenthetical statements, and making sure the Jews are sealed with the seal of the living God.

ADDITIONAL NOTES

The reason death has not yet been destroyed, is because sin and the sin nature is still present throughout the millennium, though greatly suppressed as Satan is bound these 1000 years. An act of Sin will be rare as God's judgment will be swift. (Isaiah 65: 20).

As you can see, chapter seven has many parenthetical statements, mostly the middle of the tribulation and end of Tribulation. It also touches on the millennium. It is as if Chapter seven is preparing us for coming events. The worst time of all tribulation is the last 3 ½ years. Which is called Jacob's (Israel's) trouble. *"Alas! For that day is great so that none is like it, even the time of Jacob's trouble, but he shall be saved out of it."* (Jeramiah 30: 7).

CHAPTER EIGHT OUTLINE

- ❖ The seventh seal
- ❖ Silence in Heaven
- ❖ Seven Angels
- ❖ Seven Trumpets
- ❖ Another Angel

CHAPTER EIGHT

The Seventh Seal

"And I saw the seven angels which stood before God; and to them were given seven trumpets".

(Revelation 8:2)

Chapter eight opens with a half hour of silence in Heaven. This is a mystery to many. Maybe it is the calm before the storm. I believe the seven angels mentioned in chapter eight may have been seven prophets. They were not mere humans, but *"as"* the Angels as scripture says. We will all be as the angels when taken to Heaven, again we are not to worship Angels or men. *"And I fell at his feet to worship him. And he said unto me, See thou do it not: I am thy fellow servant, and of thy brethren that have the testimony of Jesus: worship God: for the testimony of Jesus is the Spirit of prophecy." (Revelation 19:10)* The first Angel sounds the first trumpet and it would seem a meteor hits the earth, much blood was shed as a third part of the trees were burnt up. The second trumpet sounds, another meteor, mountain size falls into the sea and the sea will become blood as all sea life will die. The third Angel sounds his trumpet and another big meteor falls, its name being *"Wormwood"*. The meteor fell on a third part of the rivers and fountains of waters and, these waters will be made bitter. The fourth Angel sounds his trumpet and a third part of the sun, moon and stars will be smitten (Matthew 24:29 Revelation 6:12).We now see another Angel flying in the midst of Heaven saying three more woes are yet to come under the three trumpets to sound later. Therefore, only four trumpets sound in chapter eight.

The seventh trumpet is not the same as the trump of god in Matthew 24: 31. *"And he shall send his Angels with a great sound of "A" trumpet, and they shall gather together his elect from the four winds, from one end of Heaven to the other." (Matthew 24: 31)*

ADDITIONAL NOTES

It is clear that at the opening of the Seventh Seal, the Seventh Trumpet sounds as referenced in Revelation 11: 15, and parenthetically speaks of the middle of tribulation to the end and the beginning of the eternal kingdom to come.

The seventh trumpet brings about the beginning judgments of God, it would seem that God uses meteors as falling stars, as John would understand this vision in his time.

CHAPTER NINE OUTLINE

- ❖ The Fifth Angel
- ❖ The Bottomless pit
- ❖ Demons-Locusts-Scorpions
- ❖ Five Months of Torments
- ❖ The Angel of the Bottomless Pit
- ❖ The four Euphrates Angels

CHAPTER NINE

The Locust Demons

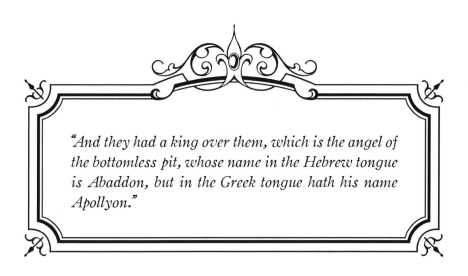

"And they had a king over them, which is the angel of the bottomless pit, whose name in the Hebrew tongue is Abaddon, but in the Greek tongue hath his name Apollyon."

This Chapter opens with the fifth trump. An angel of God opens up the bottomless pit, and 200,000,000 demons will be released. These two hundred million locusts are real, literal demons. In those days, men will seek death, but cannot die. These two hundred million locusts are real, literal demons. They will come out of the pit of hell, not some country. They cannot be killed. Their shapes show them to be beast like creatures. Ordinary locusts would not be found in the bottomless pit, nor do they have a leader. There are those who believe these 200,000,000 demons to be soldiers from China and helicopters with poison gas. Even so, it would still be 200,000,000 demons in control. (Revelation 9: 12-21). A third of men will be killed because of the demons yet, those that remain will not repent of their evil ways. Those demons will only hurt the ones that have not the seal of God in their foreheads. (Revelation 9:4) His mark or his number (666) is the number of man. Therefore, this antichrist in full power will be over the 10 nations and maybe the U. N. His name is many in number, man of sin, son of hell, beast ect…

The Sixth Trumpet sounds and four angels that were bound in the Euphrates were loosed and were trained thirteen months and twenty-five hours to slay a third of mankind. These four angels lead an army of two hundred thousand, thousand. Their power was in their tails as well as mouth, they were like unto serpents and had heads, in all this, and man still will not repent.

China now has the nuclear capability to vaporize the west coast, thanks to the gift wrapped technology of our government, as we the United States stand defenseless. We now know that North Korea also has this capability as well. I believe that more situations just as these mentioned are on the way.

ADDITIONAL NOTES

One should note, the star that fell from Heaven was an angel, for unto him the star was given, the key to the bottomless pit. Often, the word star or stars in scriptures is speaking of angels as well as men as in (Revelation 1: 20, (Pastors) Revelations 19: 10, and Revelations 22: 8-9).

According to the bible, these locust demons had a King over them. His name in Hebrew will be Abaddon, and in Greek will be Apollyon. This king was an angel which was released out of the bottomless pit, where the locust demons were. The name Apollyon means destroyer.

CHAPTER TEN OUTLINE

❖ The mighty Angel

❖ The mystery of the Seven Thunders

❖ The Little Book

❖ End Time

❖ The Mystery (10:7)

CHAPTER TEN

The Seven Thunders (Parenthetical Events)

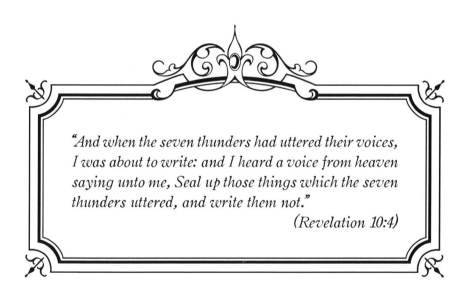

"And when the seven thunders had uttered their voices, I was about to write: and I heard a voice from heaven saying unto me, Seal up those things which the seven thunders uttered, and write them not."

(Revelation 10:4)

This chapter opens with a mighty angel (Jesus) coming down from Heaven and seven thunders cry out a mystery message that was not made known. Therefore, it is still a mystery.

Thunder references are: Matthew 17:5: voice of God, Psalms 18:13: Psalms 29:3: Job 37: 4-5: John 12:29.

The description of this angel proves it to be Jesus.

Revelation 10: 8-11. A pause here: signifies calm before the storm.

The mighty angel that comes down from Heaven clothed with a cloud, is none other than *Jesus Christ* who created Heaven and Earth? *"His feet are as pillars of fire". (Revelation 10: 1)* Seeing he could swear by no greater, he swore by himself and his Father which are one, there should be time no longer. *"The little book",* no doubt is the end of the rolled up scroll that brings an end to time as we know time. The *"seven thunders"* is just another voice or language of Heaven. Nevertheless, John was ordered not to repeat the message of thunder. We know in the days of the voice of the seven thunders and the seventh angel, when he begins to sound the seventh trumpet, the mystery of God, should be finished as declared unto the prophets of old. This is a parenthetical statement that is giving reference to the body of Christ, with Jew and Gentile, and body of Christ (the church). This does not mean the Rapture will happen under the seventh trumpet because the seventh trumpet is not the same as the *"Trump of God".* The *"Trump of God"* will rapture the Church, while the seventh trumpet proclaims what will take place the last half of tribulation. (Matthew 24: 31)

John was told he must prophecy again, in Revelation 10:10-11 other words, his life was not to end yet. Many say John will be one of the two prophets to preach in the last half of tribulation because he was told he must prophesy again. I reiterate, there is no record of his death.

Jesus said to Peter, *"What is it to you if he (John) is here when I return" (John. 21:22)* "And He said unto me, thou must prophesy again before many peoples and nations, and tongues and kings." (Revelation 10: 10-11)* Again, we have no record of John's death, only what tradition tells us. In the writings of Irenaeus it is said John died shortly after returning to Ephesus; however, this is not inspired scripture yet little reason to doubt the writings of Irenaeus.

CHAPTER ELEVEN OUTLINE

❖ Many Parenthetical Scriptures

❖ Antichrist image in the temple

❖ Antichrist over ten nations

❖ Roman religion

❖ The Mark of the Beast-(666)

❖ Armies of the Antichrist

❖ The Seventh Trump sounds (11:15)

❖ A Rapture- 2 Prophets (Revelation 11:3-12)

CHAPTER ELEVEN

Ministry of the Two Prophets

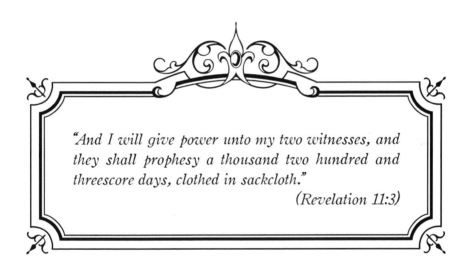

"And I will give power unto my two witnesses, and they shall prophesy a thousand two hundred and threescore days, clothed in sackcloth."

(Revelation 11:3)

Chapter eleven opens with the *"Temple of God"* being measured and the altar as well as the people that worship therein. In Revelation 11: 2 we see the outer court as well as the Holy City overthrown, and for forty-two months,(3 ½ years) controlled I believe by Antichrist forces as he dictates from his throne . He will set up his image in the temple to be worshipped, (Daniel 8: 9-14), *"the Abomination of Desolation," (Matthew 24: 15)*. Antichrist is now king of ten nations, which enables him to dictate his laws to the world. (Revelation 12:6) God's people are within themselves a nation, a holy nation scattered among all nations. Many will be called on to give their lives for Jesus Christ. I believe there is a Petra or place of protection for God's people in every nation on earth.

We are now hearing of local states within the United States (Union) looking to their constitutional right to pull out of the union so as not lose their sovereignty to the U. N. or *"New World Order"*.

Now we see the two witnesses or the two olive trees, (Zachariah 4: 1-3). The two witnesses are the same as the two olive trees. The same are called prophets in Revelation 11: 10. They prophesy 3 ½ years and are protected by God until God permits their death. (Revelation 11:15).

Are you ready to meet God? If not, why not?

> *Dear God, forgive me a sinner. I now accept your son Jesus Christ as my Lord and Savior and soon coming king. I know he died for me on the cross. I now confess my sins and ask for forgiveness for Christ sake according to Romans 10:9. I thank you Lord for saving me. Now help me to share Jesus with others. Amen.*

These two witnesses were seen in Heaven 500 years before Christ. They are called two prophets. (Revelation 11:10) Malachi 4: 5-6 reveals Elijah as one of the two, and in Genesis 5:24 Enoch is believed to be the other. Neither of these two men have yet died, and according to Hebrew 11:5, *"it is appointed unto all men, once to die and then the judgment." (Hebrew 11:5)*

The people of the east will hate these two prophets and rejoice at their death, pass gifts over their dead bodies, because the two prophets brought such conviction on their sin-filled life style, they did not want to hear God's Word.

Enoch in Genesis 5:24 was taken that he might not see death, maybe just as the Raptured Church will not see death (food for thought). Of course if Enoch, like the church, is not to see death, then he would not be one of the two prophets. The two prophets were raptured in Revelation 11: 12, near the end of the Tribulation. Moses is another possibility (Joshua 1: 1-2). We know he died as stated in Deuteronomy 34: 6, and God buried him, but why was he buried in secret. Is God somehow preserving his body as one of the two prophets? Is this why Satan disputed with the Archangel concerning the body of Moses? Why would Satan want the dead body of Moses? Maybe Satan knows something God has not let us know. (Jude 1: 9) Maybe Satan and his Antichrist will face Moses again. (Just a thought)

CHAPTER TWELVE OUTLINE

❖ Michael Casts Satan out of Heaven, to Earth
(Dan. 12:1, Revelation 12:7-9)

❖ The Wonder Woman in Heaven

❖ The man Child (Jesus) Raptured Matthew 27:52-53
(Parenthetical Scripture)

❖ The Red Dragon

❖ A great Flood

❖ A great Earthquake

❖ What about the Eagle? (Exodus 19:4)

❖ The Wilderness – (Petra-Rock City)

CHAPTER TWELVE

Two Great Wonders

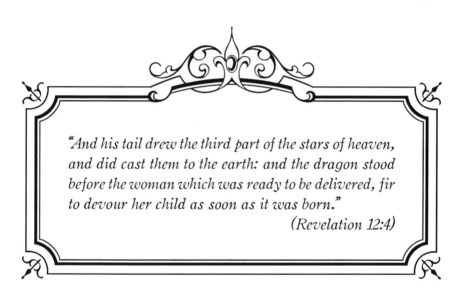

"And his tail drew the third part of the stars of heaven, and did cast them to the earth: and the dragon stood before the woman which was ready to be delivered, fir to devour her child as soon as it was born."

(Revelation 12:4)

To better understand the woman clothed with the sun and the moon under her feet and a crown of twelve stars, as referenced in Genesis 37: 9-11. The law of double reference must be applied to Mary being the woman, the man child being Jesus, the woman as the nation of Israel.

During the millennium Israel will become the Head of the *Nations of the World*, with all others under her feet. The woman, pained and persecuted at this time by Antichrist, cries out for deliverance, but before she can be delivered, she must herself deliver her man child *Jesus Christ*. This is not a tribulation rapture, rather a parenthetical scripture referring to Matthew 27:52-53. Also the Man Child could be speaking of the Remnant of Israel, the Petra Jews that will be raptured at the end of tribulation. The Dragon having *seven heads and ten horns* represents the antichrist having received power from the dragon (Satan) to become king over the ten horns (nations). Antichrist with these ten nations, seeks to devour, kill the man child, but God raptured this man child to Heaven. This causes antichrist to turn on the woman (Israel). The woman fled into the wilderness where God had a place prepared for her 3 ½ years. This place is called the City of Petra, in the land of Moab and Edom, (Revelation 12).

Also, there will be a war in Heaven, Michael and his angels will fight against Satan and his angels. Satan was cast out of heaven, and persecuted all whose names were in the Lamb's Book of Life. The antichrist and his armies will follow hard after the woman (Israel), as a flood of water, but God caused a great earthquake as in Number 16: 29-35 to swallow up his army.

In Revelation 12:4, the eagle with two wings that will fly the woman (Remnant of Israel) to safety does not have to be the United States aircraft. The eagle represents God as it did in Exodus 19: 4.

"Ye have seen what I did unto the Egyptians, and how I bare you on eagle's wings, and brought you unto myself." Now, we know God did not use natural eagles to deliver Israel out of Egypt, nor will it be necessary to use aircraft in the future tribulation to deliver Israel to safety in Petra's wilderness. God, himself will make a way just as he did in crossing the Red Sea. "To God be the glory". (Exodus 19:4)

Revelation 12: 6 teaches that this woman will flee into the wilderness, where she will stay for three and a half years into the *Land of Edom* and Moab, to the Rock City of Petra according to prophecy. For these two countries escape Antichrist see reference verses (Daniel 11: 36-45 Psalms 60:8 108: 7-10 Isaiah 16:1-5.) Now, Isaiah 26:20 reads, *"Come my people, enter thou into thy chambers, and shut the doors about thee: hid thyself as it were for a little moment, (3 ½ years), until the indignation (Great Tribulation) be over past". (Isaiah 26:20)*

The law of double reference must apply to the following statements:

First the woman represents the *Virgin Mary* who was forced to flee and hide 3 ½ years in Egypt after she delivered her man child (Jesus) (Parenthetical scripture). This man child (Jesus) was to rule all nations with a rod (church) of iron. (Isaiah 66: 7-8)

Second, the woman represents national Israel who will be the head of the nations in *"God's Earthly Kingdom".* We see the woman clothed with the sun and the moon under her feet depicted in Genesis 37:9-11. Joseph's father, mother, brothers, all bowed down to him, as all nations will bow down to Israel in the millennium. (The law of double Reference must apply here).Israel will be God's capital of the whole earth. Please take notice here the man child is not the same as the 144,000 Jews listed in Revelation 7: 4-8.The man child again is speaking of Jesus Christ. (Parenthetical scripture) (Matthew 27:52-53)

The *"Red Dragon"* represents two things: Satan as he was cast out of heaven and the woman (National Israel), who was to give birth to the man child (Jesus). Second, Antichrist as he turns on the woman, National Israel, that birth. The man child (Jesus), who was caught up to God and his throne as referenced in Matthew 27:52-53 (the man child was raptured). I believe many sinners will enter the millennial, (the ones who did not take the mark of the beast).Antichrist gather his servants to make war against Jesus Christ at the end of the Millennial? Until death is destroyed, sin or the adamic nature is still present. Therefore many will not take the mark of the beast and survived the seven years of tribulation. You surely can say they get a second chance, yet out of this people, Satan will gather together his army to face God for his last attempt to destroy God's holy people and the holy city. This is the war that ends all wars. Satan will be defeated and cast into the lake of fire. "Satan's Last Stand" Revelation 20: 7-10.

It would seem, some will sin during the millennial, and will be judged. (Isaiah 65: 20) Because death again has not as yet been destroyed.

CHAPTER THIRTEEN OUTLINE

❖ The Rise of Antichrist

❖ The Ten Nations-The Horns

❖ The Seven Heads on the Beast

❖ The other Beast

❖ The Angel from the Abyss

❖ The Deadly Wound

❖ The revived Grecian Empire of the 8th Kingdom-Little Horn
   (Revelation 13:4)

❖ Image Worship

❖ The Mark – 666

❖ His name

CHAPTER THIRTEEN

Kingdom of the Antichrist

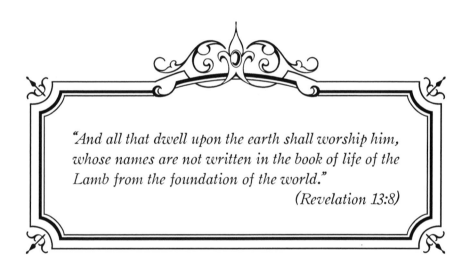

"And all that dwell upon the earth shall worship him, whose names are not written in the book of life of the Lamb from the foundation of the world."

(Revelation 13:8)

This chapter unfolds with the revelation and rise of the Antichrist in full power over the ten nations. The antichrist is symbolized by the beast with ten horns. This beast also symbolizes a supernatural spirit out of the abyss that influenced and ruled over six kings of six kingdoms in the past, Egypt, Syria, Babylon, Medo-Persia, Greece, and Rome. There remains one head on the beast that is not accounted for. This head symbolizes the seventh kingdom which will be the revived *"Roman Empire"*. The beast was also like unto a leopard which is a symbol of the eighth kingdom. (Daniel 7:6) This eighth kingdom is the revived *Grecian Empire* over which the antichrist is the king. This kingdom represents the head that received the deadly wound and was healed. Revelation 17: 11 says, *"And the beast that was, and is not, even he is the eight, and is of the seventh, and goeth into perdition."*

The Antichrist is worshipped because of his power to give life to the head that was wounded to death. This head again is referring to the Grecian Empire which antichrist will revive. Revelation 13:14 says, *"This beast is the angel out of the abyss pit"*. He will have no record of his birth, he will simply appear on the scene one day with antichrist, he will be run through with a literal sword, but of course he can't be killed. At this time, the beast will begin to put down all religions and God. He will exalt himself as God and will demand that he be worshipped. Satan here makes a last attempt to exalt himself above God; however, we will see in further studies that this attempt fails as did the first one.

Revelation 13:5 is the extent of his rule, (Seven years). He will blaspheme God and all that is in Heaven. He will make war against the saints, (Israel) and overcome them, many saints will be called upon to give their lives for the cause of Christ, and many saints will be put in captivity.

Shortly after we see another beast appear, lamb like but he speaks as a dragon, this beast causes all to worship the antichrist who healed the deadly wound. I believe this beast to be the *"Pope of Rome"*.

We see in this chapter the mark of the beast and his number (666). The number 6 falls short of God's number 7; 6 being the number of man.

The *"New World Order"*, which I believe, will be under the control of the United Nations, is the beast kingdom that will rule the world. Who is able to make war with him? And who is like unto him? (Revelation 13:4) "And it was given unto him to make war with the Saints: and to overcome them, and power was given him over all kindreds and tongues and nations" (Revelation 13:7) (Global Dictatorship).

The beginning of the extent of the Antichrist kingdoms is symbolized by the ten horns on the beast. Notice in Revelation 13:8, the word *"earth"*, should be translated land. According to the "Strong's Concordance" of the bible, page 20, number 1093 defines the word *"earth"* to have many meanings, planet as a whole, soil, region, territory, land, ground.

According to Strong's Concordance of the Bible, page 51, number 3625, the Greek meaning for the word earth in Revelation13 is land and is specifically speaking of the *"Roman Empire."* Therefore, the antichrist will rule over all kindreds, and tongues, and nations in the land or the ten nations. With these ten, he will overthrow many others, and become world ruler. With these ten nations, he will be king and *"World Leader"*. Revelation 13:11 states another beast had the appearance of a lamb, but his words were inspired by Satan himself. He will support the antichrist. This beast will be the false prophet. In my opinion, *"The Roman Pope"*, will receive great power from Satan, so he will be able to call fire out of the heavens to draw people after him. This *beast*, who I believe to be the pope, will command an image to be made of the antichrist, and that anyone that will not worship this image, should be killed. A mark will be issued to all people of his kingdom, 666. Rich, poor, free, bond, small, great, will receive this mark (emblem of the beast). Without this number, one will not buy or sell anything.

The bar code computer chips are already in use, certain people have been seen using the chip in the right hand to transact business in stores across this nation, and many major stores are now openly talking of going to a cashless system-where your money will be no good you must have this chip (mark).

Webster's dictionary defines communism *"as a theory or system of social organization based on the holding of all property in common, actual ownership being ascribed to the community, as a whole or to the state, a political doctrine or movement based on Marxism, and developed by Lenin and others. It seeks a violent overthrow of capitalism, and the creation of society"*. Wake up church, wake up America our freedom is at stake. A cashless society is one in which a select few rule, better yet, where one rules with a few he appoints under his control.

For this nation to become a communism cashless society it stands to reason the *"White House"* must be turning red. When you listen to the extreme left in Congress and some on the right fighting with all their might to change the constitution and bring about the *"New World Order"* under the control of the U. N. The word today is *"spread the wealth"*, have all things in common, overthrow capitalism, bankrupt America, go cashless.

ADDITIONAL NOTES

This supernatural spirit out of the abyss (hell) had ruled over the six kingdoms of the past, (Egypt, Syria, Babylon, Med-Persia, Greece, and Rome). It possibly was the *"Prince of Persia"* that withstood the *"Angel Gabriel"* twenty-one days until the *"Angel Michael"* came to help Gabriel to complete his mission to Daniel. (Daniel 10: 12-13).

Keep in mind, the *"Angel Michael"*, is Israel's prince (Daniel 12: 1). So it would seem every kingdom has an angel or angels assigned to them. Evil angels and heavenly angels, you have sheep nations, but also goat nations. It should be easy to know which: examples are China, Russia, and any nation that serves false Gods are ruled by these evil angels. Is America a sheep nation? I believe it is, but will America remain a sheep nation? I believe these evil angels are the ones we as the church must wrestle with and war with in getting our prayers to heaven, these are the principalities of the air. It has been rightly said, every Battle or war is first fought in the Heavens before reaching the earth, and can you see now why we must pray through. Again, we wrestle not against flesh and blood, but against principalities and evil spirits in high places. (Ephesians. 6: 12)

A Christian is as strong as his or her prayer life, praying through, which means spending time in your prayer closet with God.

CHAPTER FOURTEEN OUTLINE

- ❖ Again-many Parenthetical Scriptures
- ❖ Heaven-Mount Zion
- ❖ Preaching Angels
- ❖ The Fall of Babylon-Rome
- ❖ The Lake of Fire
- ❖ The Second Coming
- ❖ Souls under the Alter
- ❖ Armageddon

CHAPTER FOURTEEN

Preaching Angels

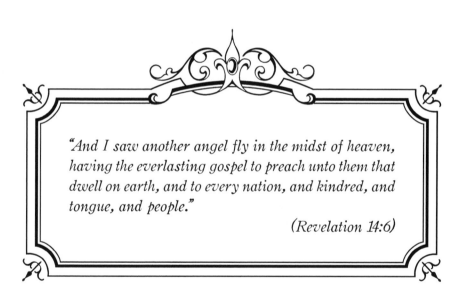

"And I saw another angel fly in the midst of heaven, having the everlasting gospel to preach unto them that dwell on earth, and to every nation, and kindred, and tongue, and people."

(Revelation 14:6)

This chapter is filled with parenthetical statements and scriptures referring to different times, mostly the end of tribulation. This chapter opens with scenes in heaven, Jesus with the 144,000 Jews standing on Mount Zion_in Heaven (the Heavenly Mt. Zion, first fruits). *"For the invisible things of him from the creation of the world are clearly seen, being understood by the things that are made even his eternal power and God-head: so that they are without excuse." (Romans 1:20)* We see the 144,000 with all of the redeemed singing a song to Jesus, that no one else can sing, not even the angel's .This would seem to be prove the 144,000 was raptured, but when did it happen? In my opinion most likely the last part of tribulation.

PREACHING ANGELS

There will be literal angels preaching in midair warning men not to take the mark of the antichrist or believe in his words. These angels will preach that all man should turn to the God who made the heaven and earth, and worship him. (Revelation 14:6)

The fall of Babylon (Modern day Rome/ America) under the seventh vial near the end of *"Great Tribulation"*. Those who take the mark of antichrist will be sentenced to the lake of fire, to be tormented day and night without rest forever. The saints that are dead at this time are blessed because they are at rest, and they will soon receive their rewards for their faithful service. This verse foretells the second coming of Christ, to fight in the Battle of Armageddon. (Revelation 14: 14-20) This verse makes this statement to be parenthetical, in that it has reference to the end of tribulation.

Just as Christ was crucified *"without the gate"*, (city of Jerusalem, Hebrews 13: 12.) is referred to as the *"winepress"* (Armageddon) in revelation 14:20, and will take place without the city of Jerusalem. The blood that is shed in this battle will be up to a horse's bridal, and will be a river of blood about 184 miles long, the greatest battle ever fought. This war ends, at the second coming of Christ. (Ezekiel 38: 21-23)

We see another Angel preaching the everlasting Gospel to all Nations, other angels as well preaching and warning all not to worship the beast or take his mark, or his number 666.

CHAPTER FIFTEEN OUTLINE

❖ A sign in Heaven

❖ Seven Angels

❖ Seven Plagues

❖ Tribulation Saints (Revelation 7: 9-17)

❖ Heaven Temple

❖ Armageddon Revelation 14: 19

❖ Jehoshaphat

CHAPTER FIFTEEN
"The Song of Moses and of The Lamb"

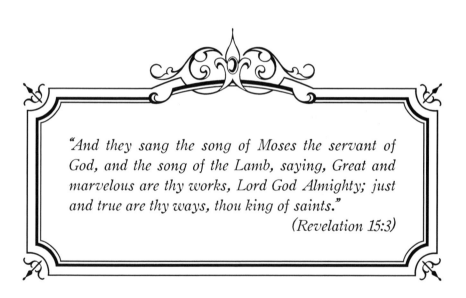

"And they sang the song of Moses the servant of God, and the song of the Lamb, saying, Great and marvelous are thy works, Lord God Almighty; just and true are thy ways, thou king of saints."

(Revelation 15:3)

This Chapter begins with seven angels that bring forth the seven last plagues, which will bring about the wrath of God. In Revelations 17:1, we see one of these seven angels showing John the judgments of the great harlot Roman religion, and this same angel is one of the seven in Revelation 21: 9 that shows John, the *"Bride of Christ"* (New Jerusalem). Later in Revelation 22: 8-9, we see one of the seven angels calling himself a fellow servant_of John and a brother, as well as one of the prophets. These seven angels were given the seven last plagues to be poured out as judgments on earth. This will complete the *"Wrath of God"* in these seven vial judgments. (This complete chapter deals with scenes in Heaven)

In Revelation 15: 2-4, John sees the tribulation saints in heaven before God's throne, standing as it were on a sea of glass mingled with fire, which represents the Holiness and Glory of God, the Father. These are the ones that became martyrs for Christ rather than take the mark of the beast. They were singing a song of victory to Jesus, as Israel once sang to Moses for their victory over the *Pharaoh of Egypt.* They all had harps. The Tribulation_Saints are Jews and Gentiles (Revelation 7:9-17).

In Revelation 15: 5-8, *"The Heavenly Temple"* is literal, just as the angels are literal and just as the tribulation saints are literal.

GOD'S THRONE

Inside this temple is the literal throne of God. The 144,000 are the ones who had gotten the victory over the beast over his image, his mark and number and they sang the *song of Moses and of the Lamb.* Many will refuse to take the mark or number of the antichrist during tribulation. The fact they sing the song of Moses shows them to be Jews, also singing the song of the lamb, shows them to be converted to Jesus Christ

ADDITIONAL NOTES

Please note just as Romans 4: 16 calls *Abraham* the father of us all, Gal. 4: 26 calls *New Jerusalem* the mother of us all. *Jesus* is the groom, and *New Jerusalem* is the bride as referenced in Revelation 21: 9-10, and the church are the children.

CHAPTER SIXTEEN OUTLINE

❖ The Seven Vials

❖ The Voice from Heaven

❖ The Wrath of God

❖ Discuss all Seven Vial Judgments

❖ Jacobs Trouble

CHAPTER SIXTEEN

The Vial Judgments

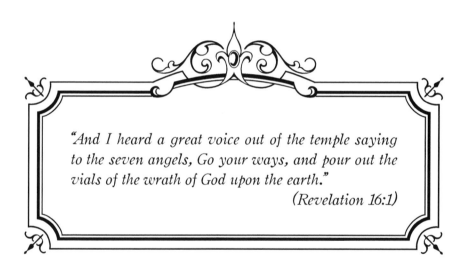

"And I heard a great voice out of the temple saying to the seven angels, Go your ways, and pour out the vials of the wrath of God upon the earth."

(Revelation 16:1)

This chapter unfolds with a voice of command to the seven angels to go their way and pour out the rest of the "*Wrath of God*" upon the Earth, "*Great Tribulation*", and continue until the second coming of Christ.

THE FIRST VIAL JUDGMENT

Under the first vial judgment, grievous sores broke out on all who had taken the mark of the beast, also on those who had worshipped the image of the beast were afflicted with these scores ("*The Abomination of Desolation*") (Revelation 16:2)

THE SECOND VIAL JUDGMENT

In this vial, we see a sea or body of water turn into blood, and every living thing in the sea died. The word "*sea*" here is in the singular meaning "*one sea*". (Revelation 16:3)

THE THIRD VIAL JUDGMENT

The angel in charge of this vial pours it out upon the fountains and rivers drinking waters, so that the waters become as blood, so that the beast worshipers could not drink from these fountains.(Revelations 16:4)

THE FOURTH VIAL JUDGMENT

This judgment brings out a scorching burning heat from the rays of the sun. The heat was so great that it caused men to blaspheme God, rather than turn from their evil ways because they knew God was in control of this judgment. Still, they would not acknowledge his glory (rightful credit) as supreme in their lives. They would not change their minds. (Revelations 16: 8-9)

THE FIFTH VIAL JUDGMENT

This judgment will be poured out upon the seat of the antichrist, which at this time is Jerusalem, where he will set up his image (Abomination of

Desolation). Also, this darkness will fill his whole kingdom (Ten Nations). Because of all these judgments, also because of this darkness, men began to gnaw their tongues for pain, and curse God who created Heaven and earth, and would not change their minds. (Revelation 16: 10-11)

THE SIXTH VIAL JUDGMENT

This judgment causes the *"Great River Euphrates"* to dry up so as to make a way for the kings of the east later to come into Palestine to cooperate with antichrist at Armageddon. This is the mission of the three lying spirits to gather these countries to the *"Battle of Armageddon."* These demons will persuade these kings to join antichrist to fight against Christ at his return. (Zechariah 14: 1-5) These spirits, from Satan, possess the antichrist and the false prophet. *"There was given him a mouth speaking great wisdom." (Revelation 16:12)*

THE SEVENTH VIAL JUDGMENT

Under this vial judgment, we see the *"Wrath of God"* coming to an end, but not until he has judged Babylon (Rome) for her sins through the ages. There was lightning and thunders which God will make known his anger and wrath. Also, Jerusalem will be divided into three parts by the greatest earthquake in the history of the nation. Great hail stones will fall from heaven about 114 pounds each, and men will curse God and walked yet in their own way. (Revelation 16: 17-19)

CHAPTER SEVENTEEN OUTLINE

- ❖ More Parenthetical Scriptures

- ❖ Two Babylon's "Mystery Babylon"

- ❖ The Great harlot Roman Religion. Even America fit the scriptures as Rome's Puppet

- ❖ The 8th Kingdom-"Little Horn"

- ❖ The Scarlet Colored Beast

- ❖ Seven Heads/Seven Mountains

CHAPTER SEVENTEEN

The Great Harlot

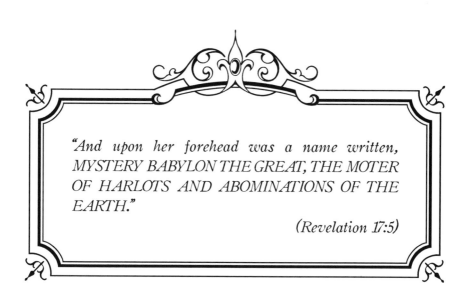

"And upon her forehead was a name written, MYSTERY BABYLON THE GREAT, THE MOTER OF HARLOTS AND ABOMINATIONS OF THE EARTH."

(Revelation 17:5)

This is a parenthetical chapter with reference to different times and two Babylon's. This chapter unfolds with their judgment of the *"Great Harlot"* which is also called *"Mystery Babylon"* in this same chapter. This *"Great Harlot"* is the Roman Religion that has its roots in ancient Babylon, where Nimrod turned away from God and built the *"Tower of Babel"*, which seems was the seat of all false religions. These Babylonian cults are found today in the Roman Catholic Church, and this is why the Roman Catholic Church is "Mystery Babylon", the *"Great Harlot"*. Very hard for me not to see America as part of this *"Mystery Babylon"*. The Bible teaches that the kings or leaders of the earth have committed fornication or spiritual adultery with this harlot or false religion, which is the Roman Catholic Church that has influenced kings down through the ages. The earth people will be drunk by the wine (teachings) of her fornications (false doctrines). In Revelation 17: 3-5, we see this woman sit upon a scarlet colored beast that is clothed in purple decked with gold, pearls, and precious stone. This woman (Rome) has a cup in her hand filled with abominations.

These colors such as gold and purple is Roman colors. The cup that is filled with abomination is the history of the Roman Catholic Church filled with sins against God. The Roman Church is drunk or filled to running over with the blood of Christians.

THE SCARLET COLORED BEAST THAT CARRIES THE WOMAN

The beast is a symbol of three things:

A kingdom which is the eighth Kingdom to be dominated or carried by the woman (Rome) or great harlot until the antichrist destroys the Harlot religion. (Revelation 17: 16) This is one of the ten kingdoms. This kingdom is symbolized by a leopard, as referenced in Daniel 7: 6: and Revelations 13: 2: 17:3. This beast or kingdom existed before John's day, but did not exist in John's day, as referenced in Revelation17: 8-11, and will be revived. (Daniel 9: 24-27) As the eighth kingdom that follows the seventh kingdom.

Now the seventh kingdom will be the ten nations formed inside the Old Roman Empire that are represented by the ten toes as stated in Daniel 2: 40-43. These kings will surrender their kingdoms over to the king of the eighth kingdom the *"Revived Grecian Empire"*. Therefore, the eighth kingdom will be made up of the seventh, which consists of the ten.

Seven heads of the beast, are seven mountains or kingdoms, Egypt, Assyria, Babylon, Medo-Persia, Greece one is in John's day, old Roman Empire and one is not yet come. Ten kingdoms revived inside the old Roman Empire.

This eighth kingdom is made up of the ten kingdoms. The Antichrist symbolized by the little horn in Daniel 7:7-8 will come out of the ten kingdoms and receive power over all ten of the kingdoms.(Revelation 17: 10) Then the 8th kingdom is formed and continues forty-two months, of the tribulation.(Revelation 17: 11, 13)

The eighth kingdom is one of the seven, and is the head that was wounded to death. The Bible says this beast, which is the *"Grecian Empire"*, John's day, but will be brought back to life (revived) in the last days as the eighth kingdom of Antichrist. (Daniel 7: 24, 25) Before John's day, five of these seven kingdoms had fallen. Egypt, Assyria, Babylon, Medo-Persia, and Greece. Therefore, one of these five must be the eight. Also, one of the five is the head that was wounded to death. The eighth kingdom will be ruled by the Antichrist and the beast out of the Abyss (pit), which is called the *Prince of Greecia*, Daniel 10: 12-21. The eighth kingdom will be the revived *"Grecian Empire"*, which was the fifth head of the beast. (Daniel 7:6) This is the head that was wounded to death. (Daniel 8:5-9, 20-25). When Alexander the Great died, as is symbolized in Daniel 11: 1-6, represents the notable horn was broken off and the Grecian Empire was divided into four Kingdoms, as symbolized by the four horns that replaced the first horn. (Daniel 8: 8). The four generals of Alexander split the kingdom. This was the deadly wound. This deadly wound will be healed in the last days when this *"Grecian Empire"* will be revived under the antichrist and beast out of the Abyss (pit).(Revelation 11: 7, 17:8) This eighth kingdom is also symbolized by the *"He Goat"* of Daniel 8:5 that was made of four kingdoms Macedonia, Thrace, Syria, and Egypt. Syria will be where Antichrist comes out of in the last days, so it seems. (Isaiah 10: 12, 14:25) Also, this eighth kingdom is symbolized by a leopard with four heads, (Daniel 7: 6: Revelation 13: 2, 17: 3)

This beast also represents a *supernatural angel* out of the Abyss (pit) that once existed before John's day as the *Prince of Persia*, he was in the

Abyss (pit) in John's day and will go into perdition. (Daniel 10: 20-21, Revelation 17: 8) This supernatural angel kills the two prophets Enoch and Elijah. (Revelation 11: 7). This was the evil angel that influenced the kings, in Daniel 10: 20-21, of the Grecian Empire before John's day, and was in the Abyss during the days of John, but will go into perdition, fill his role as the beast out of the Abyss, Revelation 13.This beast is a type of antichrist who is a mortal man. (Revelation 13:1) He receives power from Satan. (Revelation 13:2: II Thessalonians 2: 8-12-21: Daniel 8: 24: 11: 38) Antichrist will become king over the ten nations and rule the world. (Revelation 17: 12-17)

The eighth kingdom of Revelation 17: 11-13 is the same as the fourth kingdom of Daniel 7: 24 to rule the world under Antichrist: again, this is the *"New World Order"* under the control of the U. N.

These seven heads on the beast are seven past empires and called seven mountains in Revelation 17:9. Five of these 7 empires had fallen before John's day. These would include Egypt, Assyria, Babylon, Medo-Persia, and Greece. (Revelation 17:10) The sixth one, Roman Empire was in John's day. The seventh will be will be the revised Roman Empire. This empire will be formed inside the Old Roman Empire, which will be the ten horns in Revelation 17: 7. These ten nations will make up the 8th Empire which was of the seven (Greece).

These ten nations shall hate the harlot (Rome) and destroy her. The woman represents that great city (Rome). *"Mystery Babylon"* is the city that comes in remembrance before God. (Revelation16: 19) Also Babylon is called that Great City, that Mighty City (Isaiah 47: 5-7, Jeremiah 50: 4-9, 51: 4-8, Isaiah 13:1) New York City sure seems to fit the picture here as well.

Revelation 17:16-18 are parenthetical scriptures. The harlot religion will be destroyed. Then maybe, *Chrislam* will come into power. It is possible the Antichrist will be a Muslim (very possible).

In Revelation 17: 18, we see the woman being called that *"Great City"* which reigned over the kings of earth. This city comes in remembrance before God. See the following additional scriptures for reference: (Revelation 16:19, Jeremiah 51: 6-13)

You should know the reference scriptures that the city spoken of in Revelation 17: 18 is Rome. *"Mystery Babylon"* is clear in scriptures in identifying Babylon as the *"Lady of Kingdoms"*. (Isaiah 47: 5) So we see two Babylon's in this chapter. First we see *"Mystery Babylon"* harlot religion and *Rome*, the seat of the harlot religion.

A brief history of Babylon, was founded by Nimrod in Genesis 11:1-9 it reached its full glory under the reign of Nebuchadnezzar, Daniel 2: 36-38 and was overthrown under the rule of Nebuchadnezzar's grandson, Belshazzar, by the Medes and Persians and later others added to the destruction of Babylon, including *Alexander the Great*. (Daniel 2: 36-38 Daniel 5: 1-31, Daniel 8).

CHAPTER EIGHTEEN OUTLINE

❖ Babylon the Great

❖ The Great City of Rome

❖ New World Order: I believe under the control of the U. N. What do you think?

❖ The number of 666. Is it a name or a mark? Or will this be an implanted Computer Chip? I believe most likely!!

CHAPTER EIGHTEEN
Great Babylon

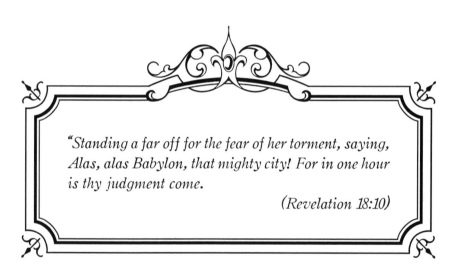

"Standing a far off for the fear of her torment, saying, Alas, alas Babylon, that mighty city! For in one hour is thy judgment come.

(Revelation 18:10)

The Subject matter is still *"Great Babylon"*, (Rome), mother of harlots and abominations of the earth and Babylon's destruction. Like most Bible subjects is debatable and filled with controversy. It is understood to be the city of Rome. Is it referring to literal Babylon, to be rebuilt only to be destroyed again? Revelation17: 7, tells us there is a mystery of the woman who is carried by the beast. If this is Babylon, where is the mystery? The mystery is found in the last verse of Revelation 17:18, *"The Great City"* which reigned over the kings of the earth. All nations and tongues are subject to Rome, even America? Has America become one of the puppets of the great harlot or *"Mystery Babylon"*? What nation is pushing the *"New World Order"* and New Age concept? We all know America is the superpower that is promoting the *"New World Order"* more than any other nation on earth. In Revelation 18:1, another Angel comes down from heaven with great power, the earth was lightened with his glory and pronounced the fall of Babylon, we are to come out of her, and trust in God alone. Soon Christians will be considered to be a threat to world peace under the *"New World Order"* with its 666 new age leaders. Now I surely do see the *"Law of Double Reference"* in Chapter 17, and 18, Babylon of old as well as "Mystery Babylon" today, Rome. Babylon's or America's fall will happen in one hour. Sounds like a nuclear blast to me. *"Vengeance is mine, said the Lord, I shall repay"* (Romans 12:19) Many believe that the one word religion will be the union of Catholicism and Protestantism as the emerging *"One World Church of Rome"* progresses as the pope of Rome calls for Protestant brothers to come back home to the mother church twisting scriptures like in John 17:22, where Jesus prayed "Father I Pray they be one, even as we are one". (John 17:22) Will this merge happen? In my opinion, "yes indeed" It is already in the works.

CHAPTER NINETEEN OUTLINE

- ❖ The great harlot (Rome) falls,

- ❖ The marriage of the Lamb (Jesus Christ) and his wife (New Jerusalem)

- ❖ Jesus returns with all his saints ready to do battle

- ❖ Revelation 11: 15. tribulation ends

- ❖ Supper of the great God

- ❖ Additional notes

CHAPTER NINTEEN

Marriage of the Lamb

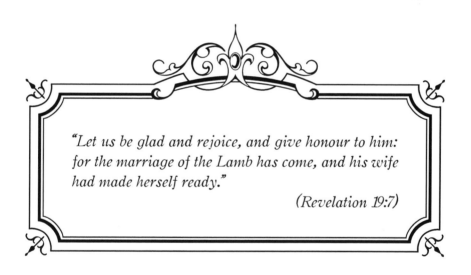

"Let us be glad and rejoice, and give honour to him: for the marriage of the Lamb has come, and his wife had made herself ready."

(Revelation 19:7)

All of heaven rejoices over the fall of the great harlot (Rome) which did corrupt the earth. This again has reference to *"Mystery Babylon"* and modern day Rome. America is Rome's puppet. The U. N. speaks for the world. The Four and twenty elders are believed to refer to the old and new covenants, twelve apostles and twelve Major Prophets. We will see in this chapter the voice of the mighty thunderings, giving God glory and honor. Therefore, thunder could be a kind of heavenly language, the Marriage of the Lamb is come and his wife (New Jerusalem) and has made herself ready. (Revelation 21: 1-2) New Jerusalem with all his saints, will be the city that is coming down in all its glory and splendor. (New Jerusalem) (Revelation 21: 9-10) We should note the word marriage is in reference to covenant relationship, just as a wife is man's glory, so is the church God's glory. John in Revelation 19:10 fell down to worship the angel, but the angel will not permit John to worship him. The angel reveals himself as a fellow servant and brother who also has the testimony of Jesus. In other words, this angel was a redeemed man of God, as were the other six before him. In Revelation 21: 9, we see the bride, the Lamb's wife already in heaven after being raptured in Revelation 4.1. Keep in mind, the bride or Lamb's wife is New Jerusalem with the church living within her walls. (Revelation 21: 9, 10) Revelation 19:11-17 is a parenthetical statement of the second coming of Jesus Christ with the church that was raptured in Revelation 4:1.

"SUPPER OF THE GREAT GOD"

"Vengeance is mine said the Lord, I shall repay." (Romans 12:19)
The fulfillment of the times of the Gentiles.
"And they shall fall by the edge of the sword, and shall be led away captive into all nations: and Jerusalem shall be trodden down of the Gentiles, until the times of the Gentiles be fulfilled." (Luke 21:24)
"But the court which is without the temple leave out, and measure it not: For it is given unto the gentiles: and the Holy City shall they tread under foot forty and two months." (Revelation 11: 2)
The last three and half of the seven years of tribulation, until Jesus returns, with the church and his holy angels (Revelation 19: 11-17) "All on white horses, to fight the battle of Armageddon in the valley

of Jehoshaphat". (Ezekiel 38-39). This will be the great supper of God. (Revelation 19: 7)

ADDITIONAL NOTES

"And I heard as it were the voice of a great multitude, and as the voice of many waters, and as the voice of mighty thunderings, saying Alleluia! The Lord God omnipotent reigns. Let us be glad and rejoice, and give honor to him: for the marriage of the Lamb is come, and his wife hath made herself ready. And to her was granted that she should be arrayed in fine linen, clean and white: for the fine linen is the Righteousness of saints. And he saith unto me, write, blessed are they which are called unto the marriage supper of the Lamb." (Revelation 19: 6:-9).

This takes place at end of tribulation just before the millennial.

The marriage supper is the same as the Passover which Jesus promised to drink new in his father's kingdom, which will take place at the interval between the end of tribulation and millennial. *"For this is my blood, of the new testament, which is shed for many for the remission of sins, but I say unto you, I will not drink of this fruit of the vine hence forth until that day when I drink new with you in my Father's Kingdom." (The millennial or earthly kingdom). Remember the Lord's Prayer, "thy kingdom come" thy will be done in earth, as it is in heaven (Matthew6:10) (Matthew 16: 28)* There is a 75 day interval between the end of tribulation and the millennial.

"And from the time that the daily sacrifice shall be taken away, and the abomination that maketh desolate set up, there shall be a thousand two hundred and ninety days (1290)."

"Blessed is he that waiteth and cometh to the thousand three hundred thirty and five days (1335)." (Daniel 12: 12)

Below you will see an explanation that mathematically breaks down the seventy-five days interval, as referred in Daniel 12:12, between the end of tribulation to the beginning of the millennial.

"LET'S DO THE MATH"

Jewish months are all 30 days in length.

Three and a half years is equal to 42 months. This leads to 42 times 30 days which equals 1,260 days.

But what of the 1,290 days and then the 1335 days spoke of in Daniel 12: 11-12.

The Passover was to be kept the second month this was the whole month or 30 days according to Jewish calendar. (II Chronicles 30: 2-4)

1,260 days equals 3 ½ years
30 days for Passover (Matthew 26: 8)
1,290 days
Then the last 45 days is to prepare all to enter the millennial
1,335 total days
"So, blessed is he that waiteth, and cometh
to the 1,335 days" (Daniel 12: 12)
I hope this explanation helps you.

CHAPTER TWENTY OUTLINE

- ❖ The Strong Angel from Heaven
- ❖ Satan is bound for 1000 years
- ❖ Tribulation Saints
- ❖ Mark of the Beast
- ❖ White Throne Judgment
- ❖ Second Death
- ❖ The Lake of Fire
- ❖ Souls Under the Alter
- ❖ The Thousand years –Golden Age
- ❖ Satan's Last Stand

CHAPTER TWENTY

Satan's Last Stand

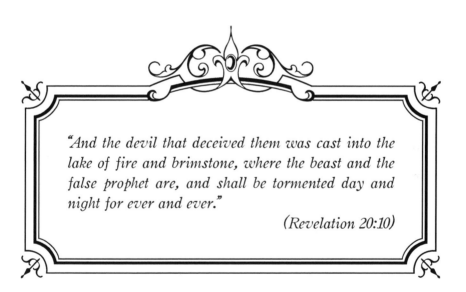

"And the devil that deceived them was cast into the lake of fire and brimstone, where the beast and the false prophet are, and shall be tormented day and night for ever and ever."

(Revelation 20:10)

After the Antichrist and the false prophet have been cast alive into the lake of fire, Jesus will bind Satan 1,000 years in the bottomless pit. After 1,000 years Satan will be loosed again for little season. Revelation 20: 4 depicts a picture of the tribulation saints that were killed for refusing to take the mark of the beast. Please take note "*In*" their hand, "*not*" on their hand. The computer chip 666 is believed to be implanted under the skin. Revelation 20:5 is a picture of the rest of the dead sinners who will be resurrected at the "*White Throne Judgment*", at the end of the thousand years that will be part of the second death. Revelation 20:6 is speaking of the rapture of the church or the first resurrection. Therefore, I believe in the premillennial second coming of Jesus Christ. In Revelation 20:7, Satan will be loosed at the end of the 1,000 years to once again to deceive the nations. These are the ones that will enter the millennium and be the nations of natural people that the church will rule over. Satan will be loosed together with his servants to fight against Christ and his servants, as Satan surrounds the camp of the saints, the "*Holy City Jerusalem*". You may rightly refer to this as "**Satan's last stand**". God himself will send fire from heaven to destroy and devour them. Satan at this time will be cast into the lake of fire, where the beast (Antichrist) and false prophet are waiting for him.

Revelation 20:11-12 depicts the white throne judgment where all the dead (sinners) stand before God to be judged by the Books, (Book of life and the Bible). Two books, a book of records and of course the Bible. Now the sea gave up the dead and death and hell were cast into the lake of fire. (Revelation 22: 12.)This is the second death. Everyone not found in the Book of Life was cast into the lake of fire.

CHAPTER TWENTY-ONE OUTLINE

❖ New Heaven and New Earth

❖ Natural People

❖ The Day of the Lord

❖ The Heavens and Earth Dissolved

❖ The Millennium

❖ White Throne Judgment

❖ Time no more—what does this mean?

❖ Beginning of Eternity for the Raptured Saints. For truly there is no beginning of eternity past or Present

CHAPTER TWENTY-ONE

"New Heaven and New Earth"

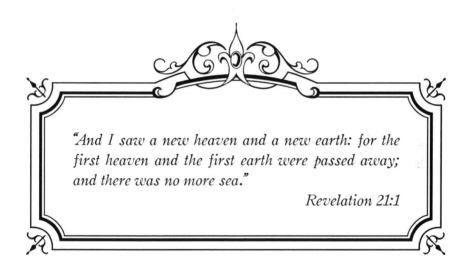

"*And I saw a new heaven and a new earth: for the first heaven and the first earth were passed away; and there was no more sea.*"

Revelation 21:1

Revelation 21:1 depicts the eternal and final state of this earth, the new renovated, purified earth, eternal abode of the glorified church. The first earth had passed away and a new renovated earth had taken place, as in the new birth, old things pass away, and new things begin. II Peter 3: 9-13 gives a clear detailed picture of the *"Day of the Lord"*. *"He will come as a thief in the night, in which the heavens shall pass away with a great noise, and the elements shall melt with fervent heat." "The earth also, and the works that are therein shall be burned up. Seeing then that all these things shall be dissolved, what manner of persons ought ye to be in all holy conversation and godliness, looking for and hastening unto the coming of the day of God, wherein the heavens being of fire shall be dissolved, and the elements shall melt with fervent heat." Nevertheless, we, according to his promise, look for new heavens and a new earth, where in dwelleth righteousness."* (II Peter 3:10-13) Also, in Isaiah 65: 17, *"for behold, I create new heavens and a new earth: and the former shall not be remembered, nor come into mind." (Isaiah 65: 17) "For as the new heavens and the new earth, which I will make, shall remain before me, saith the Lord, so shall your seed and your name remain." (Isaiah 66:22)* Yes, this will be the beginning of eternity when time will be no more.

My friend, do you know Jesus Christ as your personal Lord, and savior? If not, why not? The Bible tells us in Romans 10: 9, *"If thou shall confess with thy mouth the Lord Jesus, and shall believe in thine heart that God hath raised him from the dead, thou shall be saved." (Romans 10: 9)*. Do you believe? Have you confessed with your mouth?

"THE SINNER'S PRAYER"

Dear God: I believe Jesus Christ is your son and that he came in the flesh and died for me on the cross, and was resurrected the third day. I now believe, confess, and receive Jesus Christ as my savior.

Amen

The next event is the city of God, the holy city, *New Jerusalem*, coming down from God out of heaven, prepared as a bride adorned for her husband. Talking about special effects, Hollywood could never come up with enough special effects to match the splendor and the glory of this holy city as it descends down, and I believe slowly to a brand new earth. Yes, this is where the *"New World Order"* will begin, when all things are made new. There will be no more seas. In the process of renovation, the sea or seas were dried up. The second death is clearly understood here, as the lake of fire, the final place of the damned, as well as the devil and his angels.

THE DESCRIPTION OF THE CITY

The lights of the city will be the very presence of God himself and of course Jesus. The high wall is a type of safety and security. The twelve gates are in honor of the twelve tribes of Israel with all their names written on the gates. The twelve angels are the guardians of the twelve gates. The names of the twelve apostles are in inscribed in the twelve foundations of the city. The city is four square 12,000 furlongs or 1500 square miles. The twelve precious stones that reflect God's glory include Jasper, gold, sapphire, chalcedony, sardonyx, sardius, chrystlyte, beryl, topaz, chrisoprasus, jacinth, and amethyst are the twelve precious stones that reflect God's Glory. The twelve gates were twelve pearls. There is no temple as God and Christ are the temple therein. The nations which are saved shall walk in the light of it, and bring their gifts of glory and honor into it. Nothing unclean, or that defileth, or maketh a lie shall enter in: only the saved of the nations which are written in the *"Lamb's Book of Life"*.

The spared nations will come to bring glory and honor into the Holy City. Who are these spared people? I believe that they are the ones who refused to take the mark, number, or name of the beast. These are the leftovers of tribulation. These will be the ones who will repopulate the new earth. Will there be sinners during the millennium? Yes! Who do you think will be the ones that Satan will gather his Army from? (Revelation 20: 7-10). Why it is that death is the last enemy to be destroyed after or at the end of the millennium? (Revelation 20: 5). The rest of the dead, not all of the dead, will be resurrected at the end of the millennium, *"White Throne Judgment"*. (Ezekiel 40: -48)

"There shall be no more thence an infant of days, nor an old man that hath not filled his days: for the child shall die an hundred years old: but the "sinner" being a hundred years old shall be accursed." (Isaiah 65: 20) Yes, there will be

sinners in the millennium, there will be sheep nations, and there will be goat nations, and the Church shall rule over them, and convert many to Christ, as we rule and reign with Christ for a thousand years. (Revelation 20: 4, I Corinthians 6: 1-2)

The key word here is the *"sinner"* being a hundred years old. Now another view to consider is the possibility of conversion of all sinners prior to entering the millennial, but we know that *"sin"* will be judged during the millennial and where there is *"sin"* there are *"sinners"*.

CHAPTER TWENTY-TWO OUTLINE

❖ The River of Life

❖ The Tree of Life

❖ Healing Leaves

❖ Natural People

❖ Another Promise of Jesus-Quick Return, another Parenthetical scripture

❖ The soon return of Jesus

CHAPTER TWENTY-TWO

All Things Made New

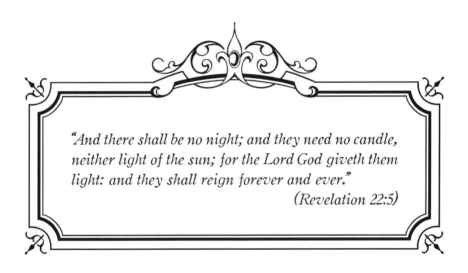

"And there shall be no night; and they need no candle, neither light of the sun; for the Lord God giveth them light: and they shall reign forever and ever."

(Revelation 22:5)

This chapter opens depicting the *River of Life*. It will run pure and clear as crystal in the new earth. On either side of the river there will be the tree (trees) of life for the healing of the nations of natural people.

In Revelation 22:7, Jesus speaks parenthetically telling us he is coming quickly. When it happens, it (rapture) will be over quickly *"Behold I shew you a mystery: we shall not all sleep, but we shall all be changed, in a moment, in the twinkling of an eye, at the last trump: for the trumpet shall sound and the dead (Christians) shall be raised incorruptible, and we shall be changed."* *(I Corinthians 15: 51-52)*

Again, I ask you, are you saved? Do you know Jesus Christ as your Lord and savior? If you would like to be born again, ask God to forgive you of all your sins for Christ sake, and ask Jesus Christ into your heart now and be your savior. Jesus died for you. Can you not, will you not live for him?

Jesus is coming soon, even so, come Lord Jesus!

The millennium is the golden age, a person of 100 years old will be considered an infant, as people will live to be 1,000 years old. A child will play with a lion with no fear of harm, the meat eating animals will all eat grass as a cow. There will be nothing that can harm anyone in this golden age, it will be as the *"Garden of Eden"*. We the church will rule with Christ for 1,000 years.

ADDITIONAL NOTES

The tree of life will be restored, no more death, sickness, pain, or sorrow. The leaves of the tree are for the healing of the nations. No more *"curses"*, God sets up his throne in *"New Jerusalem"*. The face of God, and the lamb will be the light of this city.

Well, I guess I must say concerning the natural people, that enter and repopulate the earth, what will happen to them at the end of the 1,000 years? Will they be changed, raptured, or remain an eternal natural people, we do see the leaves of the *"tree of life"* still intact after the millennial. *"And he showed me a pure river of water of life, clear as crystal, proceeding out of the throne of God and of the Lamb, In the midst of the street of it, and on either side of the river, was there the tree of life, which bare twelve manner of fruits, and yielded her fruit every month: and the leaves of the tree were for the healing of the nations."* *(Revelation 22:1-2)* At the end of the millennial reign, Satan will be loosed out of his prison to make his last stand as he gathers his army to overthrow Jerusalem. Christ will destroy Satan once and for all and cast him into the *"Lake of Fire"*. (Revelation 20: 7-10)

The *"Great White Throne Judgment"* will take place where every knee shall bow and every tongue shall confess *Jesus is Lord of Lords*, and *King of Kings*. (Revelation 20: 11-15)

The natural people of the millennial will either receive their new bodies so as to escape the next event or remain in eternal natural bodies as would have Adam and Eve had they not sinned.

"But the day of the Lord will come as a thief in the night. The heavens shall pass away with a great noise, and the elements shall melt with fervent heat, the earth and the works that are within shall be burned up. Seeing then that all these things shall be dissolved, what manner of persons ought ye to be in all holy conversation and Godliness: looking for and hasting up the coming of the day of God, wherein the heavens' being dissolved and the elements shall melt with fervent heat". (II Pet. 3: 10-12) (Reference scriptures Micah 1: 2-4, Isaiah 34: 4, Psalms 50: 3).

The next event will be *"New Jerusalem"*, the holy city, coming down out of heaven from God. "She will be adorned as a bride for her husband." (Revelation 21: 1-2)

Man's last enemy *death* will be destroyed. No more dying. Death will be destroyed. (Revelation 20: 14)

RANDOM NOTES

Worshipping Angels is forbidden Colossians 2: 10 Revelation 22: 6-9

Study the word *"Necromancy"* communication with the dead. This is forbidden in scripture.

Galatians. 5: 20

Exodus 22: 18

II kings 22: 24

II Kings 17: 17

Deuteronomy 18: 10

Leviticus 19: 26

II Chronicles 33: 6

This is really worshipping devils, as demon pretend to be angels and departed loved ones, they will get you under Satan's control and away from God's truth.

In the 1400's-1500's A.D., the Puritans, who were referred to as the Separated Ones, came to America to bring their beliefs. They contained some doctrines which were somewhat strange. Of the two groups, some seems to lean toward predestination (What will be, will be) there is not much hope or comfort there.

What stands out to me in the 1600's, is the King James translation of the Bible, the most challenged, as so it seems. When Satan fails to destroy the word of God in the person of Jesus Christ, who is the word of God, John 1: 1, he will then set out to destroy God's word in print. With so many translations available, this also will fail. Heaven and earth will pass away, but God's word will never change. (Matthew 5: 18). My personal preference is King James translation.

In the 1700's Jonathan Edwards was a great revivalist of his time. Another man greatly used by God was George Whitefield. This was the time of the Great Awakening. There was also John Wesley, who traveled by horseback preaching the Gospel. He was the founder of the Methodist Church.

In the 1800's we think of the Plymouth Brethren, which was an Evangelical Movement that can be traced to Dublin. There was also, J. N. Darby (the Darby Bible), and many, many more Great men of God. It would serve all Christians well to research the history of all these great men of God.

Then there was the *"Azusa Street Revival"* in Los California in 1906, which was led by William J. Seymour, an African American preacher. The Pentecostal movement which is characterized by miracles, speaking in tongues, and healings that were like a great awakening in America. In our day, we have a great falling away of "many false prophets bringing strange fire to God's alter and spiritual death to God's people", as predicted in the scripture Matthew 24: 24. Just turn on your TV and judge for yourself.

TYPES, NAMES, AND TITLES OF THE ANTICHRIST

The Assyria	Isaiah 14: 4
King of Babylon	Daniel 7:8
Little Horn	Daniel 7:8
Gog	Ezekiel 38-39
Prince	Daniel 9: 26, 27
King	Daniel 8: 23
Man of Sin	II Thessalonians 2: 1-12
Wicked one	Isaiah 11: 4
Beast	Revelation 13
Spoiler	Isaiah 16: 1-16